Understanding Industry

Second Edition

J M Baddeley, MA(Ox

Butterworths

LONDON BOSTON
Durban Singapore Sydney Toronto Wellington

in association with The Industrial Society

First published 1980

Second Edition 1983

© The Industrial Society, 1983

British Library Cataloguing in Publication Data
Baddeley, J.M.
   Understanding industry. — 2nd ed.
   1. Great Britain — Industries
   I. Title
   338.0941   HC2566
ISBN 0-408-10860-6

Typeset by Butterworths Litho Preparation Department.
Printed and bound in England by The Whitefriars Press Ltd,
London and Tonbridge

Foreword

The challenge of the future lies in striving to make the best possible use of the world's resources. The need to conserve energy and protect the environment is well known. But the challenge of harnessing the most important resource of all, the gifts and energy of people, is often neglected.

In the last decade we have spent too much time arguing about how to divide what is available. We have forgotten that we cannot spend what we have not earned, nor consume what we have not made. We must understand that our future depends on our ability to pay our way, so that we can improve the quality of our lives, do more for the sick, have smaller classes in our schools, increase our help for the two thirds of the world which is starving and much more.

New technology — inventions such as the microprocessor — is giving us unbelievable opportunities to create a better world for all to live in. If we are to play a valuable part in this new life we need to find out all we can about industry and commerce. We must take every opportunity to go into factories and offices and experience at first hand the challenges of production, communication and supervision we will find there.

In this way we can learn how working life can be made better and more enjoyable for people and how they can be more effective in what they are doing.

For it is these people, those working to create the goods and provide the services we need and to create the wealth to pay for our schools, hospitals and social services, in whose hands the future of our country is held.

This is both a challenge and a great responsibility.

Author's Acknowledgements

This book owes much to many people, some acknowledged, others not. Thanks are particularly due to the following for their help and advice.

Allied International Designers
APE—Allen Limited
BOC Limited
Careers Research and Advisory Council (CRAC)
Cranfield Management School
Department of Industry
Design Council
Esso Petroleum Company Limited
Financial Times
Ford Motor Company Limited
Fulmer Research Institute
Hills Road VI Form College, Cambridge
IBM United Kingdom Limited
Imperial Chemical Industries Limited
Institute of Marketing
Institute of Personnel Management
J. Walter Thompson Company Limited
The Leys School, Cambridge
Lloyds Bank Limited
Long Road VI Form College, Cambridge
Malvern College
Marks and Spencer Limited
Mars Limited
May & Baker Limited
Metal Box Limited
Netherhall School, Cambridge
Peter Symonds' College, Winchester
Rowntree Mackintosh Limited
Sevenoaks School, Kent
Shell U.K. Limited
Sherborne School
Solartron Electronic Group Limited
Tower Housewares Limited
Transport and General Workers' Union
Trades Union Congress
Tube Investments Limited
United Biscuits (UK) Limited
University of Bradford, School of Science and Society
University of Cambridge, Engineering Department

   I should like to thank Laurence J. Haylock for drawing the cartoons and sketches.
   Finally I must thank my husband and parents for their patience, encouragement and support, and my children for their adaptability, without all of which this book would not have been written.

Publisher's Acknowledgement

Without the Industrial Society's close involvement with, and support of, this project; without their extensive help, valuable advice and friendly co-operation, this book would not have been possible.

Notes

Where the pronoun he (or she) is used in this book it covers both men and women, either of whom could be found in the jobs and situations described.

The job profiles and examples included in the book are of real people, real products and real companies. The case studies, simulations and exercises are, however, based on fictitious organisations and any resemblance these may bear to real companies is unintentional.

Contents

Introduction

Defining industry

When we talk about industry we refer to a vast network of different enterprises making goods and providing services for the community and, in Britain, employing some 20 million of its people.

These enterprises are as diverse as they are numerous. No two companies are the same. Some are massive conglomerates, others small one-man bands; some make goods, others sell them; some are in cities, others in the country; some operate underground, others on the sea. Some jobs are dirty, others clean; some are intellectually stimulating, others physically taxing, and so on.

But varied as industry might be, when considering it we are faced with an inescapable fact: today's society cannot live without it. Industry provides the goods and services we demand; it helps to pay, through taxes, for the health service and our schools; and it supplies us with jobs.

For industry cannot operate without people, all sorts of people: salesmen, accountants, fitters, typists, operators, drivers, scientists, managers, engineers and clerks. And it is these people — the way they work, the problems and challenges that face them — that this book is about.

Types of company

One of the difficulties in defining industry is that different people give the word different meanings. Some see it as a term which implies only manufacturing. In this book, however, it is used much more broadly. Industry is seen as encompassing mining, construction, transport, retailing, banking, entertainment and many more — everything, in fact, except Government services like the armed forces, local authorities and hospitals.

Having said that industry is almost impossible to define, we need to classify companies along some sort of lines in order to build up a picture of what business is all about. We can broadly group companies into three main types.

- *Manufacturers* make goods such as cars, clothes, steel, ships, biscuits and bandages. Linked to this group are the extracting companies which manufacture their finished product from raw material they have removed from the ground or, perhaps, the sea.

- *Retailers* specialise in selling goods others have made. Examples of retailers are department stores, shops and supermarkets.

Cortinas on Ford's production line at Dagenham

• *Service companies* provide services both to other firms and to individuals. Examples of service companies are banks, insurance companies and travel agents.

Although there are common features within each of these groups the businesses are as diverse as their products.

Manufacturing companies are usually organised into three main areas which work together to ensure that the right goods reach the right customers in the right quantities at the right time at the right price. These departments are finance, which organises the supply and use of money; manufacturing, which makes the goods; and marketing, which assesses customer requirements and sells the finished goods.

In a retailing organisation the manufacturing function is performed by an outside company whose products are purchased to be sold by the retailer to the customer. In this case marketing assumes a whole new dimension — that of store management. In a service company the function of manufacturing becomes the providing of the required services.

In all three types of business nothing can be done without the money necessary to buy machines, pay rent and wages, etc. Also the goods and services the company can supply must be brought to the attention of potential customers and must meet their needs.

These main areas are backed up by a series of other service functions, such as personnel management, which must all work together to keep the enterprise as a whole running efficiently and profitably.

Company size

In a small company — one with only 30 employees, for example — several of the different functions may be performed by a single person. There may be a company secretary dealing with finance, administration and personnel matters. The managing director would probably be personally responsible for marketing. Most of the people working for the company would be directly involved with making the goods or providing the service.

In a large firm the organisation is far more complex, though the principles on which the business is run are much the same. Senior managers responsible for large departments of specialised staff report to the managing director. Because the need for specialisation is greater, employees in large companies are more restricted in the variety of tasks they can perform as part of a single job, but their opportunities for promotion are probably greater.

In the big corporation there is often a number of separate, subsidiary companies grouped together under a central holding company. Each subsidiary will have its own organisational set-up, with policies being made by a complementary structure at head office, which may also provide specialised services and advice to the satellite companies.

Company ownership

Another way of grouping companies is by their form of ownership. If you were about to set up a business, you could do so in one of three ways:

- As a sole trader
- In partnership
- As a limited company.

Sole trader If you operated as a sole trader, you alone would be responsible for running the business and alone would receive the profits, regardless of whomever else was involved or employed in the firm. You would be self-employed and if the business owed money you would be fully responsible for paying its creditors. Examples of businesses likely to be sole traders are newsagents and garage owners.

Partnership You could form an association with one or more others — a partnership. All partners share responsibility for managing the business and share the profits. If the business experienced financial difficulties all the partners would be liable in this case for the debts.

Limited company If you set up your business as a limited company, you would register it under the Companies Act and be subject to its restrictions. In law you would be forming a corporation. In a limited company, as the name implies, the amount of money the shareholders can be forced to pay out to cover the company's debts is limited, usually to the value of their shares when they were originally issued. It is only the owners' personal liability which is limited. If the company goes bankrupt, all its assets — land, buildings, equipment, stock and so on — must be sold to pay off its debts, but its shareholders only have to pay up to the legal limit of their liability.

The Companies Act requires limited companies to supply certain information about, for example, shareholders, directors, assets and mortgages annually to the Department of Trade, as well as a copy of the accounts.

A limited company may be either

- *Private* (also called *unquoted*), where its shares are held by a group of from 2 to 50 people (excluding employees) and can only change hands by agreement between them. An example is C. & J. Clark Limited, the shoe manufacturer.
- *Public* (*quoted*) where its shares can be bought and sold freely on the Stock Exchange and may be owned by individual investors, pension funds and other companies, provided only that there is a minimum of seven shareholders. Examples are ICI and Marks and Spencer.

There are two other groups of companies which, perhaps, deserve special mention.

- Nationalised industries are created by Acts of Parliament and are owned by the public as a whole through the state. Examples are the British Steel Corporation, British Railways and the Post Office.
- Profit-sharing companies where shares can be either owned by the employees or held in trust for them. An example is the John Lewis Partnership.

Whatever the legal form of a company the principles on which it operates remain the same. If it is to be profitable it must be able to produce and sell goods and services to its customers and not be continually seeking outside aid. Whether the business is owned by a group of individuals or the state, it still relies on its employees doing their jobs effectively for its success.

The organisation of the book

Part 1

As shown above there is no such thing as a 'typical' company which can be described in detail. Part 1 of this book, therefore, sets out to outline the general sort of organisation that might exist in a medium to large-sized manufacturing company. Examples are given to illustrate how this may vary in different types of business.

Inside a large Marks and Spencer store

The basic structure consists of a managing director with six senior managers — each controlling a separate department — reporting to him. These departments are

- Marketing
- Research, development and design
- Manufacturing
- Finance
- Personnel
- Management services.

Each chapter gives an outline of the responsibilities of the department and some examples of people doing the type of work involved. These are followed by some case studies, simulations and discussions on different aspects of the department's activities. The section ends with two practical exercises designed to give an insight into the formation and operation of a company.

Part 2

No company of whatever size, shape or form can operate without people. Part 2 looks at a series of issues concerning those employed in industry and the part the companies play in the society in which we live. Finally we look at the way British industry may develop in the future and the effect this may have on those working in it.

The banking hall of Lloyds Bank's Hanover Square branch

Part 1

Marketing

Outline of the function

Marketing forms both the first and the last link in the chain of a company's operations. The marketing department must establish what the customer wants before the product can be designed and manufactured. Once it is made, it is their responsibility to see that the product actually reaches the customer.

The marketing manager (or, as he is often called, the marketing director) is a member of the senior management team reporting to the managing director. Under him are groups of specialists manning the following functions.

Market research

This involves studying the market to find out what the customer — perhaps the housewife, for example — really needs. Market researchers must find out as much as possible about her likes and dislikes, the performance she is looking for and the price she is prepared to pay, before the company spends large sums of money on making something which will not sell.

Product planning and development

This section follows up the market researcher's findings by developing new products, analysing the cost of making them and designing packaging for them. Often this is carried out by a separate research and development department such as that described in Chapter 2.

Advertising and promotion

If customers are going to buy a product they must be made aware of its existence and advantages. The advertising section communicates with the customer through media such as newspapers, television, the cinema and posters. It also handles sales promotion by means of special offers, display equipment in shops, competitions and product-launching campaigns. Many

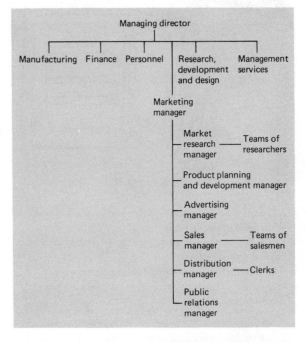

companies use the service of professional advertising and sales promotion agencies for these tasks rather than employ large numbers of highly specialised staff in an area in which the work load will fluctuate.

Sales

The sales staff deal directly with the all-important customer. This is usually the largest section in the department with several sales managers responsible for teams of salesmen. These teams may each operate in a different geographical region, or some may work on exports and others on the home market. Their jobs involve

- Developing and maintaining personal contact with the customer, often a large retailer;
- Keeping the customer informed of new products,

changes to existing lines, prices and promotional aids such as display cards;

- Providing technical advice to the customer and answering questions;
- Demonstrating and selling the product;
- Providing after-sales service and dealing with any problems that may occur.

In addition there may be brand managers responsible for co-ordinating the selling of specific ranges of goods. goods.

Distribution

It is the responsibility of the distribution section to make sure that the goods sold are delivered to the customer on time. It may operate a fleet of lorries and possibly deal with shipping agents and airlines.

Public relations

Sometimes a separate department in its own right, public relations is concerned with maintaining the company's image in the community. This activity can have significant effects on the popularity of its products, as people are more likely to buy from a company with a good reputation. Public relations work involves preparing

press releases, producing company magazines and organising conferences and sponsored events.

The nature of the jobs in marketing will depend to a certain extent on the type of customer and the type of product. A salesman in one company may be selling sweets to newsagents, while another spends his time persuading managers of major industrial concerns that new £100 000 computers will make their companies more efficient.

The main groups of product salesmen deal with are

- Industrial products, such as manufacturing machines and chemicals, which are sold to other companies;
- Consumer goods, such as washing machines, food and clothes, which are sold to the public through retailers;
- Services, such as banking and insurance, which have to be sold to both companies and individuals.

The marketing department must work closely with other sides of the enterprise if it is to be successful. It has to liaise with the manufacturing department to see that production schedules meet demand; with the finance department to set prices and establish what revenue is available for advertising and promotions; and above all with the research and development department to see that the designers and researchers are kept constantly in touch with market requirements.

Retailing

Retailing needs special mention, for it is a rather different sort of marketing. Shops provide a vital link in the marketing chain as manufacturers seldom have the means of selling their product directly to many millions of customers. In fact, 45 per cent of all British consumer spending goes through retail outlets, such as chain stores, department stores and mail order companies, which employ some 2½ million people.

In retailing the store manager is the central management figure with responsibilities ranging far more widely than those of the marketing manager. He is accountable for everything that goes on in the store and all the people who work in it. Managers in charge of the various store departments, such as clothing and kitchenware, report to him. His job, therefore, is very much bound up with managing people, while manufacturing industry's marketing manager will have relatively few staff under him. The store manager also deals with other administrative matters such as security, stock control and accounts.

A key position in retailing is that of buyer. Whereas his counterpart in a manufacturing company is telling the production manager what and how much should be made, the retail buyer has to predict what is going to sell, and buy it from outside.

A buyer forecasts the demand for his product as much as 18 months ahead. He then finds a supplier and negotiates the price. He must be flexible enough to organise supplies to cope with both sudden unexpected booms and equally dramatic falls in customer demand.

Profiles

Simon Tuckey, product group manager, United Biscuits

'Our target was £7½m. It wasn't easy, but we passed it.'

This is how Simon Tuckey, a product group manager with United Biscuits, looks back on a recently successful marketing campaign.

Simon joined United Biscuits after taking a degree course in business studies. During his training as a student he spent six months in production at their Harlesden factory.

'I had thought that no one could get seriously involved with making a packet of biscuits. Too ridiculous. Then I saw a huge industrial machine for the first time, 3000 people, all that machinery, producing so much . . . and the problems of control and organisation!'

He spent time working in finance, distribution, personnel and export marketing.

'After that lot I was raring to go. Then they put me in the sales force for a year. It's like a cold shower . . . pleasant in retrospect. Now when I'm making my strategic recommendations I give serious thought to the poor so-and-so who has to go out there and do it.'

In his first marketing job, although he worked with his brand group manager, he also had plenty of freedom to operate on his own initiative. There Simon was given the job of re-launching the Crawford's Christmas range which consisted of several middle-of-the-road brands. 'The range had been dawdling along for some years without much significant impact on the market or the company', he says.

The product had to be revamped, with the assortments changed to suit new consumer tastes, and a new shortbread was added to the range. New admin systems were developed to cope with the expected increase in business and to increase efficiency.

'The first phase was packaging. New designs for packs were worked out and approved. Next came in-store displays — what opportunities were there, what display material do we need, how could we persuade the stores to do what we wanted?

'Then we organised a sales force promotion — a big presentation with every aid, including a specially made film (produced jointly with the sales training people), to motivate the sales force and explain the campaign.'

And in the end it was all worthwhile. The £7½m sales target for the four-month Christmas period was not only met, but passed.

Robbie Halkett, national accounts sales manager, United Biscuits

Robbie Halkett's job in sales in United Biscuits involves working under Simon's 'cold shower' the whole year through . . . and he enjoys it.

'In sales you are as near as you can be in a big company to being your own boss. You have a target to achieve and it largely up to you how you organise yourself to meet it. You travel a lot and have to deal with many different types of people. Successes and failures are instantly recognisable, so ups and downs are part of your life. You also have some detailed paperwork to do — but then no job is perfect.'

As national accounts manager with the food division in Glasgow, Robbie is responsible for dealing with the very big customers who buy in millions of packets.

'The biggest problem is money. It's easy to buy your way into a market, offering bigger and bigger discounts than your rivals, but we have to make profits not just volume.

'I have an annual target to achieve — £3m this year — and to help me achieve it I have a promotional budget to "spend" with my accounts. The main part of the job is to use this money to get the best possible return in terms of sales turnover.'

Robbie keeps in close touch with his customers.

'The people on the other end of the 'phone are marketing directors, chief buyers — people with a big say who are well informed. They are interested in negotiating profitable business. They appreciate what is important, and what isn't doesn't worry them.

'You may laugh at the product, but selling nuts, crisps and snacks doesn't bother me. People like them — they must do because this is one of the fastest growing markets in the food business.'

Bob McNinch, sales representative, IBM

Bob McNinch is a sales representative for quite a different product. He works in the general business group of IBM, which markets small and medium-sized computers and office products such as photocopiers and word processing machines — typewriters with built-in memories.

It is a demanding job calling not only for considerable technical knowledge of the product, but also for experience of dealing with customers and working out specific solutions to their problems — often acting as a type of consultant.

Bob, like Robbie Halkett, enjoys the fact that he is very much his own boss.

'I could stay in bed every morning and no one would be any the wiser if it wasn't for something called "self-discipline" telling me I'd be sorry.

'The work capacity of the job is enormous. I'm working until 7pm most nights and snatch a quick sandwich lunch, but when you get a couple of good days it's the greatest feeling in the world. You have worked hard, sweated hard, you've been in a lot of situations where you have had to think hard, and at the end the contract has been signed and you feel great.

'Believing in the products I sell helps an enormous amount. I can see them doing good.'

What is it that keeps Bob working such long hours?

'I am paid more than I spend, so money has ceased to be a major motivating factor, though it was at first. I think it is the achievement of being good at something that's important to me. When the sales figures come in at the end of the month, I know — and everybody else knows — whether I have done my job well.

'IBM is an enormous company, but they try their best to know you and good communications help you to feel that the top of the tree is not so far away that you're not going to get a chance to sit on it. Although you're on the lower branches it is still within climbing distance.'

Bob thrives on the pressure. 'If you had time to sit down and think about it, it might worry you, but everything moves too fast for that.'

Francis Ball, merchandiser, Marks and Spencer

When Francis Ball goes shopping he buys shirts by the thousand dozen. As a merchandiser at the head office in London of Marks and Spencer it is his job to ensure that the company's stores are supplied with a regular flow of the right types and sizes of shirt of a consistently high standard of quality and value.

'Merchandisers are responsible for ensuring their department's profitability. This means negotiating prices with suppliers, working out margins, and making sure that all our plans work when they're put into practice. We'd lose money if we didn't meet the demand for popular lines, and we'd waste it if we made too many of a slow seller.'

A great deal of co-ordination is required to ensure the smooth flow of supplies at Marks and Spencer. The spring range is planned in March of the previous year. The selector — called a buyer in many companies — works in the same department as the merchandiser under a merchandise manager. He first sifts the fashion ideas from his colleagues and the suppliers and interprets them as specific garments which can be sold in hundreds throughout the chain of stores. A technologist then checks that the fabric and make-up specifications are up to standard. Next the merchandiser decides how much cloth to buy, which suppliers

will make what, how many they will make and when they will do it.

While this is going on, the Marks and Spencer merchandiser is also keeping a close watch on current production programmes, making sure the manufacturers have all the necessary components, monitoring sales, and, if need be, altering production schedules.

Francis co-ordinates the work of manufacturers to meet the needs of the stores, and to do this he needs to know

exactly what is going on in both. 'It is no good giving a big allocation of a popular line to lots of stores if adequate supplies aren't available,' he explains.

Marks and Spencer has 10 shirt suppliers with 21 factories, and they each give him a detailed run-down every fortnight of what they've made, what fabric they've got in stock, what they've dispatched and what they're about to make. The final stock allocation for each individual line is made jointly by the merchandiser and the distribution manager.

Francis, who was an aeronautical engineer before joining Marks and Spencer, also has to liaise with the export department to co-ordinate the production of shirts for overseas customers.

'If an export customer makes a specific order he quite rightly expects to get it unchanged. We have to pull out all the stops to make sure he does, otherwise we may lose his business in the future.'

As far as the home market is concerned, Francis spends much of his time visiting stores and suppliers to keep in close touch with their needs and problems. The success of the company's buying policy depends on teamwork, and a merchandiser in one of Marks and Spencer's hundred different buying departments is very much at the centre of the team.

Launching a new product — marketing example*

In 1976 Rowntree Mackintosh launched the now-familiar Yorkie chocolate bar with such success that within two years it had captured a 20 per cent share of sales in this highly competitive market. This meticulously planned marketing coup has played a major part in pushing the firm into leading position in the total UK confectionery market.

Sales of bars of chocolate had been steadily declining since the early 1970s. The rising price of cocoa had forced companies to make their bars thinner, in order to maintain the size of the surface while keeping the price stable. This did not seem to be popular with customers.

* After an article in *Journal of the Institute of Marketing*, November 1978

New product successes in chocolate are rare, but Rowntree Mackintosh decided on a strategy of aggressive marketing by means of continually adding to its brand range. The company regards the two most important criteria for selecting new products as the size of the market and its own existing share. That is why, in the early 1970s, Rowntree found particular interest in the chocolate blocks sector of the market. At that time the sector was big, about 70 000 tonnes, and the company's share was relatively small. Cadbury's Dairy

Milk had been — and in fact still is — leader in this field, but its sales were declining.

So Rowntree Mackintosh spent several years carefully researching the market opportunities and looking at the existing products — their sales volumes, the main market trends, consumer attitudes to existing brands, advertising claims, reasons for switching brands, consumer perceptions of differences among them and the use of different pack sizes. They augmented existing data with further qualitative research to obtain a clear understanding of consumer motivation, tastes, needs and satisfactions.

As a result of this research five new product concepts were devised by the company and its advertising agency J. Walter Thompson. Each was tested on four groups of consumers who tasted them under the observation of a market research agency. Four out of five concepts were discounted, but one showed a good deal of potential.

It was called 'Rations' and was designed as a thick, sustaining bar associated with open-air activities. The advertising theme would have suggested that it should be eaten 'when you've got to keep going' with, for example, pictures of mountaineers eating 'nourishing' Rations. It was intended to fill a gap in the market for a solid, thick block of chocolate.

Consumers, however, criticised the connotations of war-time austerity invoked by the name Rations. The presentation suggested mere utility without enough implication of enjoyment. So more ideas were developed based on the same theme but with more attractive presentation. Eventually the whole image of the brand was refined. A series of new names and wrapper designs was created and underwent rigorous consumer tests. Of these 'Yorkie' proved to be the most popular.

The launch strategy was just as carefully planned and implemented. The company realised that Yorkie could be quickly and easily imitated and so a decision was taken to launch it in a substantial area of the country — about 25 per cent. From the experience gained there they assessed the necessary production rates and stock holding in order to be able to extend rapidly to national distribution.

Before selling began, national account managers and sales managers had attended a conference at which they were carefully briefed about the product. They were then able to prepare and motivate the entire sales team for the mammoth selling task ahead. This was so successful that every major customer accepted Yorkie.

At a separate national sales conference the company's field salesmen were given the full information on market analysis, objectives and research behind the Yorkie launch. They were also supplied with the full range of selling aids.

It was vital to achieve rapid, high distribution to take maximum advantage of the television advertising that accompanied the launch. The company therefore planned a 'commando-like' exercise which resulted in more than 90 per cent of all retail confectionery outlets being supplied within 20 weeks. Salesmen were asked to report their success stories back to head office, and these were published to maintain enthusiasm among the sales force.

The specific consumer demand met by Yorkie was for something satisfying and sustaining to eat. It was therefore crucial that it should offer competitive value for money in terms of the amount of chocolate per penny. Because it is so thick its surface area is considerably smaller than that of its competitors, but it is also heavier — a fact which justified its slightly higher price. Distributors were encouraged to eat Yorkie themselves, and this convinced them that it was good value and further stimulated sales.

Yorkie still faces the continued problem of escalating raw material and production costs. Nevertheless the launch demonstrates the ability of good marketing to challenge the apparently unassailable leaders in the market and carve out a substantial slice of sales. And in spite of the difficulties of the confectionery market at present, in the words of the television advertisement, 'Yorkie keeps moving on' — towards greater sales.

Class activity

Summertown Containers Limited — case study*

Summertown Containers Limited is the engineering division of Marsden Agricultural Producers Limited, one of the largest companies of its type in the United Kingdom. The division was specifically formed some 20 years ago to service the stainless steel tanks and containers used in handling milk and milk products.

In 1960 it began to develop and fabricate stainless steel containers for use in agriculture and related

* This case study was provided by the Cranfield School of Management.

activities, and then, on request, to custom-build for other users of this type of equipment. By 1965 it was selling stainless steel containers throughout the United Kingdom, as well as exporting into continental Europe. Three years later it had developed so rapidly that a full field sales force was established covering most of Western Europe. The industry consisted of about ten major producers and a number of smaller ones.

The problem

According to the sales manager, Summertown Containers had grown to be one of the 'top ten' mainly as a result of its highly competitive pricing policy. However, the competition has become extremely vigorous of late, especially in product innovation, although the Summertown engineers have so far been able to place a close substitute on the market soon after each competitive innovation.

Summertown has always placed great emphasis on technical service. Its origins were as a service organisation, and company managers believe that their success in the market place has been based upon their reputation for providing customers with individual attention. Indeed, many of Summertown's sales staff have been with the company from its early days and were originally service engineers.

The Summertown sales division is organised into regions with sales offices in Tunbridge Wells, Bath, Northampton, Malvern, Ripon, Lancaster and Edinburgh. The salesmen are extremely active and effective in terms of sales contacts, customer relations, dispersion of product information and obtaining sales.

Whenever a need arises for a new type of container or a modification to an existing model, the sales staff contact the design engineers at the manufacturing plant in Lancaster. The design engineers supply a preliminary design and cost estimates to the sales staff, so that specific details on capacity, size, cost and so on may be shown to the potential customer. The design engineering department is manned by a staff of very competent engineers versed in the various technical areas needed to design stainless steel containers. Recently there have been numerous complaints from the engineering department about the methods of the sales staff.

The problem came to a head when the sales staff returned with a large order for a radically new type of container. The engineering department had previously provided preliminary designs and cost estimates to the sales staff, but the sales staff announced that what they had sold had little relation to the preliminary designs. Indeed, it was completely different.

The complaints of the engineering department were summarised by the chief design engineer:

'The sales staff come in here and ask us for a preliminary design for a new container, and we break our backs to provide them with the information at very short notice. Then they have the gall to come back and tell us that they have sold a completely different container, for which we have done no work. It seems to me that they will sell anything the market wants, instead of what we design for them.'

Another point of irritation to the engineers is the salesmen's habit of bargaining on the prices of containers with each customer. The chief design engineer's comment on this practice was 'Hasn't anyone around here ever heard of a standard price?' Finally he observed:

'They seem to sell just whatever they please. Some months we stand idle waiting for business to come in and at other times they rush us off our feet. We go onto excessive overtime and even then let down half the customers who've been given impossible promises. They all come on the 'phone to us and we end up acting as a PR department. It's time someone sorted them all out.'

Discussion

You are the marketing director of Summertown Containers. Consider the following points:

(1) What, in fact, is the problem and why are things going wrong?
(2) Does the fault lie with the sales staff, the designers or both?
(3) What would you do to remedy the situation?

Advertising

One of the most controversial aspects of marketing is advertising. It is sometimes accused of being 'deliberately misleading' and persuading innocent television viewers to waste their hard-earned money on poor products they do not really want. People complain bitterly that they pay for the vast sums of money spent on advertising in the price of the goods they buy. How much of this is true?

Included here are some extracts from a publication of the Institute of Advertising Practitioners explaining what they think advertising should do; some quotes from the British Code of Advertising Practice which controls the conduct of advertisers; some figures showing the money spent on advertising in this country; and an example of the way one company used a television advertising campaign and its effects on the company's image and sales.

WHAT ADVERTISING DOES

What advertising can do

There are a number of things that advertising can achieve, and very effectively.

Advertising develops a direct bond between producer and customer. In many cases this franchise is more valuable to a company than its physical installations. If machinery is damaged, it can be repaired or replaced. If the public reputation of a company is destroyed or allowed to lapse, the business may never recover.

Advertising is, in a very direct way, a form of guarantee that the product or service it promotes will deliver value to its users and maintain its standards. No rational businessman invests money in advertising unless he is convinced that what he offers to his customers is of sufficient worth to command a continuing market. Should he discover this is not the case, he ceases to advertise and the product is withdrawn.

Advertising ensures that people are aware that they have a choice to select what they want in a wide range of purchases, and to reject those which are inappropriate to their lives. Individuals are very different. A product which is eminently satisfactory to one housewife may not be given houseroom by another. In a free society, both must be given the opportunity to suit their own preferences, exercise their

own judgements and cast their own votes for the brand by buying or refusing to buy. Encouraging such choices develops customer discrimination.

Advertising is an essential part of competition, and competition is essential to choice. Every day, advertising demonstrates that it can sell an enormous range of products and services to millions of people, to the benefit of the countless businesses that use it. This advertising stimulates increased production (and therefore employment), and the economies of scale which help to stabilise prices and encourage wide distribution. It also encourages manufacturers to compete through product improvement and innovation, offering better products at better value.

Advertising not only increases sales for individual companies, but also expands total markets. Convenience foods, freezers, hi-fi equipment and holidays abroad are examples of products and services that have ceased to be for a favoured few and have become widely available and widely used.

Advertising maintains the independence of the press and broadcasting media. Income from advertisements keeps media independent of government influence, and makes a wide and varied choice available to the public at lower cost. Without this advertisement income, the reader would pay a great deal more for a smaller, less colourful publication, and commercial television and radio would disappear altogether.

What advertising can't do

Advertising cannot get repeat business for a product or service which does not represent real value to the consumer. The greater the amount of advertising put behind poor value items, the larger the financial loss to the advertiser. The consumer decides.

Advertising on its own cannot always make instant sales. It takes time to build a business and a reputation. So it is important for advertising to be continuous.

Advertising cannot sell things which are not available in the kinds of shops or outlets where consumers normally expect to find them. Only in rare cases could

advertising succeed in encouraging a housewife to search for a particular product and accept no substitute.

The cost of advertising

Advertising costs money, as do capital, manpower, raw materials, packaging, transport and all the other essential parts of the manufacturing and marketing process. The funds apportioned to advertising are concerned with creating and maintaining markets for the goods produced.

Without advertising as a method of achieving volume sales comparatively quickly, the very expensive business of launching new products and services would be greatly limited, and those which saw the light of day would be very expensive. It is only when sales have reached certain levels that large-scale production, packaging and distribution are economic propositions. When this happens, prices tend to come down, or quality or quantity is improved, or all these combine, to the benefit of the customer.

Truth in advertising

There are a number of laws and statutory instruments which control the content of advertisements. Far more important to all those working in advertising — whether for advertisers, agencies or media — are the stringent requirements of the self-regulatory controls embodied in the British Code of Advertising Practice.

The Code has two functions. For those in advertising, it lays down criteria for professional conduct and the maintenance of high standards. For the general public, it defines the self-imposed limitations to which those using or working in advertising must conform.

The Code complements the law. It is more easily adaptable to changing social and economic conditions and can act faster to stamp out any dubious practices. It can also control areas which defy legal definition: questions of taste and decency, for example.

When breaches of the Code occur, advertisers are quick to amend or withdraw the advertisements concerned. Should they not, media agree not to sell them advertising space or airtime, and they would risk unwelcome publicity by the Advertising Standards Authority which publishes regular reports of its investigations.

In the case of television commercials, every film must be approved for transmission before it can be screened, to ensure that it complies with the Independent Broadcasting Authority's code.

In practice, it is clearly in the interests of advertisers and their agencies to ensure that potential customers are neither misled nor disappointed by a discrepancy between an advertisement's promise and the product's performance.

Source: After a booklet by the Institute of Practitioners in Advertising entitled *What Advertising Does*

Extracts from the British Code of Advertising Practice

All advertisements should be legal, decent, honest and truthful.

All advertisements should be prepared with a sense of responsibility to the consumer.

All advertisements should conform to the principles of fair competition as generally accepted in business.

No advertisement should bring advertising into disrepute or reduce confidence in advertising as a service to industry and to the public.

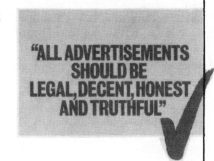

Total Advertising Expenditure in the U.K., analysed by medium

	£ million 1964	£ million 1969	£ million 1974
Press (newspapers, magazines, etc.)	288	387	649
Television	102	129	203
Poster and transport	18	21	34
Cinema	6	6	8
Radio	2	1	6
All media	416	544	900

This includes expenditure by all advertisers, for example the Government, private individuals and companies.
Source: Advertisers' Association Annual Surveys

Advertising Expenditure as percentage of Gross National Product, 1974

Country	%
U.S.A.	1.24
West Germany	0.90
U.K.	0.80
Switzerland	0.70
Spain	0.52
France	0.39

Source: J. Walter Thompson, Advertising Expenditures in Western Europe 1960 to 1974.

SO WHAT DID WE GET FROM OUR TV COMMERCIAL?

John Newsome, Dunlop's General Advertising Manager, discusses the aims and achievements of their recent corporate advertising campaign on television.

That tennis-playing girl losing most of her clothes on peak-time TV has done a lot to underline Dunlop's place on the map. But she didn't just spring from the court into nation-wide fame without preparation.

Over more than 20 years Dunlop has, from time to time, run a number of advertising campaigns aimed at telling people what we do and this counts as 'corporate' advertising, rather different from the more familiar and frequent advertisements aimed to sell particular products like tennis balls, tyres, shoes or Dunlopillo mattresses.

In fact, from the early 1950s to 1973 — a time when we were expanding rapidly — the company ran a number of advertising campaigns in the national press to explain what Dunlop did. But it was only after this, in 1974, that we set about explaining to customers and investors that Dunlop was not quite what they thought it was.

The reason for this heavy and sustained burst of advertising was to improve people's view of the company in order to make a better climate for the sale of *all* Dunlop products.

We did this because, at the end of 1974, we learnt that many people had confused and inaccurate ideas about what Dunlop did and sold. Questioning the public, market research teams found that we were known mostly as tyre makers.

Very few people recognised Dunlop as makers of all the vast range of our products. The questioners also found that we were not regarded by the public as a forward-looking or dynamic company.

Correcting the picture

Worried that these views of Dunlop might put off potential customers and investors who put up the money for the business, we set about correcting the picture.

Based on the reports of outside views of the company, we planned a campaign of advertising to put the record straight and show to the world that we were a company which was *modern, technological, diverse, international, exporting* and *profitable*.

In 1975 and '76 we began with a campaign in the more expensive newspapers and specialist magazines. This was aimed at impressing the investors and the 'opinion makers' — like MPs and journalists, along with our major industrial customers.

By the end of 1976 there was plenty of evidence that this campaign was going well. The general opinion of the company was much improved, especially among those at whom we had been aiming the campaign — the decision takers and opinion formers. It looked as though our aggressive advertising in the press had made its impact.

Cheered by this success, we decided to enlarge our target audience to include everyone: not just the newspaper and magazine readers, not just the influential hundred of thousands, but the millions of TV viewers who account for almost all Dunlop's customers.

The message was simple: Dunlop products are essential to many sides of everyday life: 'You'd be surprised how much you'd miss Dunlop'. The best way of getting this message to the largest number of people was clearly on TV.

The campaign itself is now history. Our advertising agency hit on a joke — the 'vanishing' rubber dinghy, wellington boots, tennis-umpire's ladder and, of course, those tennis clothes.

At the Cannes Film Festival the jury took time off from ogling the starlets on the beach to give the Dunlop commercial a 'Golden Lion' award for TV ads. And apart from all the friendly chat about the truly memorable minute's worth of TV, the agency concerned used a 'still' from the commercial to advertise *themselves*.

After all the praise though, we still had a tough question to answer: was the campaign on which we had spent a great deal of money achieving what we had hoped for? Had the commercial sold the product?

On the evidence of more questions to the public, the answer was 'Yes'. First the number of people claiming to be aware that Dunlop was advertising its style was up three-fold. And most of those who had seen the ad could remember the main sequences.

Getting the right answers

What was the message of those sequences? The viewers had come to feel more strongly that Dunlop made 'a wide range of products' which were 'used every day'.

And the company was more widely recognised as 'technologically advanced' and making 'an important contribution to Britain's export earnings'.

Asking people about Dunlop after the TV ad produced answers which showed they now thought of us as making a more varied range of products and some of them knew a good deal more about what this range of products included.

These responses to more market research came at the end of last year. Since then the commercial has had another airing on TV with a few changes in the scenes and Dunlop's image, as reported from market research, has improved even more. One professional who measures these things for a living, now rates Dunlop's image as second to only one company in the U.K.

This reaction, along with press comment and the views of the public, suggests that our TV advertising campaign has gone far to meet its objective: improving the company's image and thus creating a much better climate for selling all the goods of every division which carries the Dunlop name.

We have had evidence already that putting Dunlop on TV has helped to sell the goods. We've made millions smile and we intend to keep them smiling — and buying our goods.

Source: Dunlop News, June 1978

Discussion

Consider the following questions.

(1) Could soap powder be sold as effectively in brown paper bags, with no mass media communication to advertise it? List the advantages and disadvantages of this simple method of selling and evaluate them to see if the consumer would benefit from its use.

(2) Could an advertisement persuade you to buy something you did not want? How often have you bought something because it was reduced in price or had a competition or special offer attached and then regretted it?

(3) Choose ten television, radio or cinema commercials or magazine or newspaper advertisements. How many of these are really misleading? In what way do they misrepresent the facts? How many inform you about the product and help you in deciding whether to buy it? Which would you describe as 'good adverts' and why?

(4) What are the advantages and disadvantages of the different media for advertising to the customer? If you worked in an advertising agency that had a number of different clients, which medium would you recommend for selling the following: cars, ladies' underwear, insurance policies, beer, fertilisers and holidays? What would be the reasons for your choices?

(5) A significant percentage of television and radio time consists of advertisements. What do you consider to be the essential ingredients of an effective and entertaining advertisement? Choose a product and try writing, or ideally recording, a 60-second radio commercial to advertise it. The adverts can then be acted out, or played back, and discussed.

the sales managers asked 'Why do the senior managers always do the tasting?' 'Because they know how to make biscuits' was the reply.

Class activity

The wholesome biscuit factory — simulation

Who knows best?

Management at the Wholesome biscuit factory, near Maidstone, was eager to expand its range of products. Every month the marketing department would meet with the research and development department and organise a tasting of samples of the new recipes they were considering for production in the bakery.

At the tasting would be the managing director and his management team. If they felt that one of the new biscuits would sell in the shops they would bring it into production, ask the company designers to come up with some attractive packaging, advertise it and distribute batches to their retailers.

The problem

Unfortunately Wholesome did not seem to be having much luck with its new lines; the customers just did not want to buy them. By the time this was discovered, however, considerable amounts of time and money had been spent in altering production schedules, purchasing packaging material and advertising.

After a particularly bad flop, the marketing manager called a meeting of the key men in his department to decide what should be done. At this meeting one of

Discussion

If you were the marketing team of Wholesome, what strategy would you adopt to remedy the situation?

Experiment

A practical experiment may illustrate the problem. Select four different biscuit recipes, ranging from one which is inexpensive to make to one that has a high proportion of extravagant ingredients such as butter. Bake one batch of each biscuit for the correct time at the correct oven temperature. Next bake one batch for slightly longer and perhaps in a hotter oven so that the biscuits are slightly browner than would be considered perfect in the best catering schools. Label the sample batches.

Form two groups of tasters: one comprising 'cooks' who know the recipes and one those who were not involved in the baking. Ask the groups to award the biscuits points on a scale of 10.

Discussion

(1) Do those who know how the biscuits were made have the same preferences as those who do not?

(2) In what way may this be relevant in marketing?

Research, Development and Design

2

Outline of the function

In order for the manufacturing department to be able to make what the market wants there must be a group of people who design the goods that translate consumer demand into reality. In many companies this is carried out by a separate department known as research and development (R&D), design or, perhaps, product planning.

This department usually consists of a relatively small number of specialists under a senior manager. Its work covers two main areas:

- Industrial design, which is concerned with the appearance of the product and the way people use it.
- Engineering design, which looks at product performance.

It holds a whole pint of milk and costs only £14.50 to make

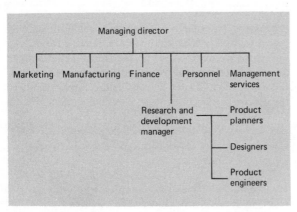

The designers must balance out three — sometimes conflicting — factors. They have to achieve a good design that meets the requirements of the customer and can be produced at a price the customer is prepared to pay. It is no good inventing a perfect product which the manufacturing department cannot make at a reasonable cost and for which there is no particular market anyway.

The R&D department is concerned with all stages of product development. They produce ideas for new products, or modifications to existing ones, and investigate the feasibility of producing these designs commercially. They may be involved in designing the interiors of offices or factories, determining fashions in clothing or preparing material for advertisements. Here are some examples:

- In the *food industry* R&D would develop new brands and better methods of preparation; test these — first in the laboratory, then in a pilot plant — and finally introduce them into production.
- The *packaging industry* makes plastic-coated boxes for the sale of ready-cooked foods. Before these

could be put onto the market, teams of researchers had to decide on the best material to use for the plastic lining; develop the process by which this is stuck onto the box; investigate manufacturing, filling and closing methods; analyse production costs; and ensure that the product would fulfil strict hygiene requirements.

- In the *motor industry* the designers may produce drawings of a new model. These would show not just the appearance but also the detailed engineering in which factors such as fuel economy and safety would have been considered. They would then build a prototype for testing. Meanwhile their colleagues in the planning section would be analysing market research data and looking at manufacturing capacity and cost to determine whether the product were technically feasible, competitive in price, aesthetically pleasing and a viable proposition in terms of investment and profitability.

- In the *chemical industry* R&D may be concerned with discovering chemical processes for making new products in a laboratory, and adapting these methods for the manufacture of thousands of tons — efficiently and cost effectively — on a commercial scale.

The R&D department has to come up with not only the new products but also new, improved production processes and machines to manufacture these products. It must meet the company's continual demand for faster, more efficient assembly, greater accuracy and quality and reduced costs. Design work in industry is essentially practical in nature. Organisations cannot afford to spend hard-earned profits on pure research for its own sake. They need their designers to arrive at feasible solutions to real problems, and to work in close co-operation with all the other departments of the company which will be involved with implementing these solutions.

Profiles

Jack Izatt, chief design engineer, Solartron

Dr Jack Izatt is chief design engineer at Solartron, in Farnborough, a company which specialises in the design and manufacture of instruments and sophisticated electronic systems such as radar simulators used in training radar operators.

Solartron has remained at the forefront of this highly competitive field by emphasising and investing heavily in research and design. This has enabled the company to offer tailor-made solutions to its customers' problems, while maintaining economic costs.

Jack is in charge of several teams of five or six engineers, each team working on a different project. He says

'Teamwork is an essential part of the job. It takes at least two people to make anything useful, and even when there are a thousand engineers working on the design of one aircraft, they're still grouped into small teams with project leaders.'

The first step in the design process is for the designer to find out what is required by the customer. He then looks at what is already available, because the solution is seldom the development of an entirely new product, but more commonly an important modification to

an existing one. 'There are so many spin-offs from each product, and often a small change can lead to a completely new application,' he explains.

Choosing the right product is essential to its success.

'For this the designer needs two things — creativity and academic ability. It's no good having one without the other.

'The work of a design engineer is more like that of a sculptor than a scientist.

The sculptor makes a sketch and then makes a model, but the final article is produced from a mould and this is normally done by other people. The only difference is that the engineer has to design something useful. He sketches his design, making models and experimenting to see that the plan will work. Having chosen the best design his job is finished and he is left with a huge pile of papers saying what he wants done.'

As with all jobs in industry, there is a strong element of co-operation with people from other disciplines with different skills. Jack spends more than half his time talking to people from other departments in the company.

'Engineering is mainly about people, persuading people to do things. So much of my day is spent talking — to technicians, draughtsmen, production engineers, purchasing department people — and considering the commercial side of the products which we are designing for the markets of the world.'

In the electronics industry design has changed at terrific speed and the development of the new microelectronic technology has created all sorts of new opportunities for the design engineer.

'Not long ago we were all talking about valves, but now it has changed beyond recognition.'

But working in such a rapidly moving environment can be extremely satisfying.

'We get tremendous pleasure from making

our first models, playing with the design, and then seeing large numbers coming off the production line and thinking: "I designed that . . . that's one of mine." '

David Baird, senior research chemist, ICI

Dr David Baird is a senior research chemist at the research department of ICI's Organics Division in Manchester. This division makes up about 10 per cent of ICI, and one of its major businesses is manufacturing and selling dyes for a variety of textiles. David's job is to help keep ICI's dyes up-to-date by inventing new ones, making them and having them tested. He has this to say of a typical day — if such a thing exists in this type of job.

'I try to spend a few minutes planning my day and discussing progress with the junior chemist who works with me. He does most of our experimental work with only occasional guidance, and we have to make sure we are both working towards the same objectives. Thereafter what I do tends to depend on the priorities for that particular day. I am chemist-in-charge of my laboratory of five people and have responsibility for its safety, equipment and day-to-day running.

'Rather less than half my time is spent on practical chemistry, although this is still the aspect of the job I like most. Currently I am working on reactive dyes for cotton. These are organic dyes which form a chemical link with the cloth during the dyeing process and which are therefore very unlikely to come off while it is in use. The dyes all have to be soluble in water, an important property for manufacturing industry, since water is by far the cheapest and safest solvent to use.

'The experimental procedures themselves are usually fairly simple and to a large extent these days we carry them out using automated apparatus which requires very little supervision. However, experience and ingenuity are needed to decide the reagents, temperatures and other conditions which will make what we want efficiently. Once prepared, the product usually has to be isolated — this can be a problem — and then we have to make sure of its structure and decide on its purity. Our analytical section helps us with that.

'A very important part of my job is to decide what dyes I want to make. I have to find out what properties are required from my colleagues in the technical service department, which tests the dyes. They are in direct contact with our customers all over the world and know what methods they use and what their problems are with existing dyes. They might tell me, for example, that a cheap red dye is wanted, which needn't be very bright, but must not fade when the fabric is used in a chlorinated swimming pool. I would then have to translate these technical requirements into chemical terms and to decide what sort of dye may have the right proporties and be cheap enough.

'A lot of my ideas will be generated in discussions, both formal and informal, with the 250 or so other chemists in the research department, about a hundred of whom work in dyestuffs. They represent an enormous pool of experience on which I can draw. There are also many other scientists, both here and elsewhere, whom I consult, usually by telephone, and several times a year I will visit a

factory, a university, another ICI division or attend a conference somewhere.

'Another big source of ideas is our library, with its thousands of books, journals and patents, and I spend probably 10 per cent of my time there. It also has access to several computerised data bases all over the world, and if I want some specific information, I can search these more or less at will by a direct telephone link.

'In the dyestuffs field patents are very important. I can use them to find out what ICI's competitors are doing, and I can also patent inventions myself. This is a complicated procedure involving a lot of paperwork and experimentation, but it is worthwhile because where a patent is granted to us, only ICI can use the invention.

'I enjoy my job and will probably spend the rest of my career doing it. The opportunities for promotion are quite good; it is possible in ICI for even a very senior man to be a scientist if he so desires, rather than a manager of scientists, and it is this sort of job which I would ultimately like to do.'

Development of a new product: a surgeon's helmet — design example*

A major factor in the success of an operation involving bone surgery is preventing infection from the surgical team coming into contact with the exposed bone surface. An eminent hip surgeon conceived the need for enclosing each member of the team in an individual suit in order to reduce contamination to the patient. From this original concept he developed the idea of a complete face helmet to be worn under a gown enveloping the entire body. Filtered air would arrive in the operating theatre and stale air would be removed through pipes attached to the outlet of the helmet.

His knowledge of the essential requirements for the helmet allowed him to make a mock-up with materials readily at hand in the hospital workshop. But to develop the idea further the expertise of technologists with knowledge of a wide range of alternative materials and processes was needed.

The surgeon contacted the Yarsley Research Laboratories where the technologists and designers examined all the critical features required. Firstly they needed to know the main functional requirements of the helmet: it had to be robust, cleanable and anti-static. Secondly they considered the personal aspects: it needed to be visually attractive, have pleasant tactile

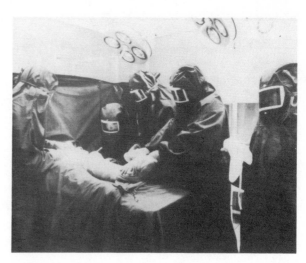

The helmet in use in the operating theatre

qualities, and be comfortable for the wearer for several hours.

In addition the helmet would need to allow good visual and audio communication. It would also have to be compatible with the gown and able to be attached to outlet tubes carrying exhaled air.

The technologists then considered all the available materials and decided that a plastic would be most suitable. Eventually one was selected that had the appropriate mechanical qualities — fairly tough and not too rigid. The helmet could be produced by a moulding process that would give the product a high gloss finish, and the materials and tooling costs would be acceptable for the numbers envisaged.

As well as selecting the material, the method of production had to be considered and the most suitable was injection moulding; this is the process of forcing melted plastic under considerable pressure into a metal mould.

The production engineers then decided how to mould the helmet bearing in mind the high cost of manufacturing metal moulds and special technical problems. They decided to make the helmet in several pieces and to assemble the separate components with adhesive. When they came to consider the detailed design of the components, certain technical complications meant that the original specification would need to be altered to accommodate the moulding process; the changes were agreed, moulds were made, and a small number of prototype helmets were produced for field trials. From the results of the first trials, further modifications were made before the final product was manufactured for sale.

The newly-designed surgeons' helmet

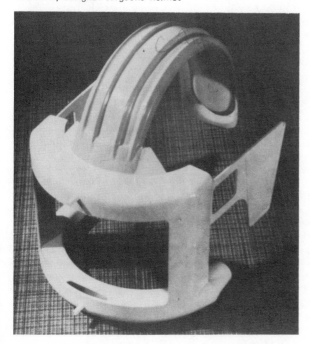

---

* This example and the following exercise were provided by the Fulmer Industry Education Project.

Class activity

FIE Packaging Company — classroom design exercise*

This exercise traces the development of a product through the design stages to meet the requirements of a customer. The project can be carried out in a similar way with any product of your choice. This case is based on a comparatively simple example, and a few relevant facts, such as costs, are given. If you choose to work with other types of product, the relevant data should be available from manufacturers in industry, but it is recommended that the example chosen should not be too complicated.

The exercise

As members of the research and development department of the FIE Packaging Company, you have been asked by a customer to develop packages to contain one-pound quantities of biscuits and to present them with drawings or prototypes and price quotes.

(1) Define the project

Any design project has constraints, such as cost and time for completion. List all the questions FIE would have to ask the customer in order to establish the objective of the project.

(2) Consider the solutions

What is the product required to do and in what ways can this be achieved? At this stage do not worry about how practical the solutions are. Simply list every idea which arises; consider possible shapes, sizes and materials. There are four ways you can go about this:

- Look critically at all the existing solutions to the problem.
- Come up with some original creative solutions of your own.
- List all the logical solutions.
- Use trial and error.

(3) Select the most suitable solution

Now you need to look closely at all the solutions you have listed to determine how practical they are. Evaluate their advantages and disadvantages; consider the constraints that were set by your definition of the problem; look again at the function the product has to perform; and eliminate all but the most satisfactory solutions. Remember that the product must meet various requirements, such as to protect the contents from breakage, possibly to advertise them, and to keep them fresh. You must weigh up the relative importance of these different functions to see which design will best meet the customer's requirements.

Breakdown of Costs for FIE Packaging Company for 10 000 containers

Company costs	Metal £	Plastic £	Paper £
Design	800	1 000	600
Materials	200	100	30
Manufacturing	350	100	150
Distribution	50	30	30
Overheads	300	300	300
Total	1 700	1 530	1 110
Profit (15%)	255	230	166
Selling price	1 955	1 760	1 276

(4) Materials and processes

Having established the basic design of the package, you should then decide on the material it should be made of and the manufacturing process. The relative cost of certain materials, given in the table above, should be considered.

(5) Prepare drawings and manufacture prototype

If possible you should make examples illustrating the advantages of the alternative solutions to show to the customer. Alternatively you could prepare a series of drawings. Consider the colour and external appearance of the design and the materials available, as well as its shape and assembly.

(6) Selling price

This may be of major concern to the customer. Add together all the costs which have been incurred in preparing the design, the expected manufacturing costs and the FIE profit margin. This will give a price at which the customer will be able to purchase the goods.

(7) Presentation to customer

You should now have a number of solutions which you can present to the customer. Arrange a five-minute demonstration to show him the advantages of the various designs over one another and comparative costs. From this brief explanation he can select the design which best meets his needs at a price he is prepared to pay.

The importance of design to the future of British industry

If British industry is to be lifted out of the doldrums over the next few years, it has to compete more effectively with its trading competitors, for example, Germany, the United States and Japan.

The following extracts are taken from a speech made by James Pilditch, chairman of Allied International Designers, who sees design as a key factor in this competition.

Innovation versus invention

At the moment we are losing our market share. Nine out of every 10 dishwashers we buy are made abroad. Nearly half of all washing machines and three-quarters of all audio equipment are imported. This means loss of revenue, and loss of jobs.

Total imports of finished manufactured goods cost us £8853m in 1976 — more than the National Health Service (£6169m), more than all education (£7000m). These imports — largely of goods we ought to be making ourselves — cost every household in Britain the equivalent of over £9 a week.

The priority for action therefore is clear: to provide products people in this country want to buy and can buy in preference to any other. So, what is the secret? Years ago an American millionaire was asked how to get rich. He replied in six words —

FIND A NEED THEN FILL IT

These six words sum up the difference between invention (at which we excel) and innovation (at which we need to). Innovation is the whole process by which new ideas and processes are translated into the economy.

Concorde is a good invention, if one thinks of the engineering genius in that plane. Is the Boeing 747 as brilliant, as novel an invention? Maybe not. But nine Concordes have been sold (with five more on option). Four hundred and six Boeing 747s have been sold. One has earned about £270m; the other at least £8120m. The 747 moved a new idea into the economy, Concorde has not.

Here is an example of how modifications of a design converted a need into reality.

Ever Ready, now called Berec, used to make a lamp for motorists. It was a solid, square object designed originally to take a big square battery. Now the designers could certainly have restyled it . . . changed the colour, altered the handle and so on. But the real problem was different. The big square battery was not in universal distribution.

Often the batteries had been in stock so long, they had lost some of their power.

That was the first problem. Because the lamp is so bulky, where was it kept? In the boot where it bounced around. *Not surprising if connections worked loose and failed when you wanted them.* The third problem was that foreign competition was cheaper. Manufacturing cost of any replacement was bound to be a worry.

Here's what the designers did. First, they redesigned the lamp to take ordinary batteries available everywhere. Second, at the expense of the swivelling beam, they made the lamp flat. Now the handle moves to form variable legs. So now it fits in a glove compartment.

Third, they simplified the manufacturing process to attack costs. The old lamp had 72 parts and 49 assembly operations. The new lamp has half the number of parts and only 28 assembly operations. It costs 25 per cent less to make. With an improved profit margin it meets the price of comparable imports.

WE ARE LOSING SHARE OF OUR HOME MARKET

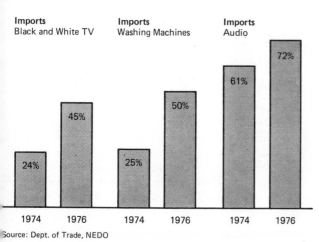

Imports
Black and White TV

Imports
Washing Machines

Imports
Audio

1974 1976 1974 1976 1974 1976

Source: Dept. of Trade, NEDO

WE ARE LOSING REVENUE
UK Consumer Electronics Market

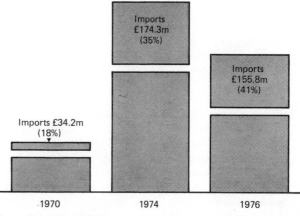

1970 1974 1976

Source: Dept. of Trade, NEDO

Has this development been successful? Yes. In its first year domestic sales have more than doubled and, according to the company, are definitely eating into imports. If we take sales of the old lamp as 100 per cent, first year sales of the new lamp in the U.K. were 223 per cent. Forecast sales of the new lamp are 357 per cent.

Why is it beating foreign competition? Because Ever Ready has clearly given people what they want. The interesting thing is that they knew before they made it. They analysed the market. They had the product redesigned to meet a clear brief. Then they used models to test the new proposition. When the time came for investment, they knew they were on the right lines.

Source: After an article in *Time and Tide,* November 1978

MOTORMATE EVER READY SALES (GROWTH RATE)

OLD

NEW

	old lamp	*new lamp*	
		1st year	forecast
UK	100%	223%	357%
Export	100%	952%	3810%

Discussion

(1) To what extent do you think that the future of British industry lies in the hands of its designers?

(2) How might we go about improving our design output so that more people are prepared to buy British goods rather than imports?

(3) What other factors prevent people 'buying British'? How might these be remedied?

Manufacturing

3

Outline of the function

At the core of any manufacturing company are those who actually convert raw materials into finished products. This is done by the manufacturing department, which often employs the bulk of the workforce. This department must co-ordinate the factory's demands for its three main resources: labour, materials and machines. Optimal use must be made of all three while the standards and services required by the customers are maintained. The methods of production are always changing and the jobs call for flexibility and rapid decisions.

The department is headed by a senior manager — the works, manufacturing, or, perhaps, factory manager — who reports to the board or managing director. He may have under him two managers heading the two main subdivisions of production and engineering, or he may control both of these himself.

Next in line will be managers in charge of each shift, and then foremen supervising the production operators, fitters, electricians and other craftsmen. Traditionally those who actually made the product and those who looked after the machinery involved were divided into separate departments — production and engineering. Nowadays it is accepted that co-operation between these two groups is essential to the efficient running of the factory and they are more often under a single department.

The main manufacturing functions are

- To carry out production schedules to meet agreed targets
- To see that quality is maintained in the manufacturing process
- To control carefully costs and minimise waste
- To maintain the machinery used in production, both that directly involved in making and packing finished goods and that in support systems such as heating and ventilation
- To install new equipment when required.

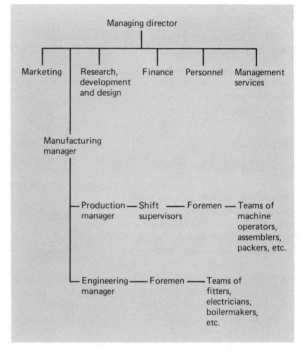

To execute these functions satisfactorily manufacturing must work closely with other departments of the company, particularly

- Marketing, which provides input on customer requirements
- Research and design, which develops new products and production processes
- Personnel, which sees that the manpower needs of the factory are met
- Finance, which controls the budgets.

Also part of the manufacturing department may be such other aspects of production as work study, distribution of materials and finished goods and stores, where supplies of raw material and parts for equipment are kept.

Although the managers and supervisors in the department have almost invariably some technical qualifications and experience, they are also important members of what is called line management. This means that they have responsibility not only for the technical side of the job, but also for the employees working under them. These key line managers are often in charge of large numbers of people, and will be involved with communication, training, consultation, promotion, deployment of labour and negotiation. In fact they often spend their time not so much on technical matters as on ones concerning people.

In many modern factories the production process has been progressively automated so that it is now capital rather than labour intensive. At the same time much effort has gone into improving working conditions on the shop floor by reducing noise levels, heat, dust and similar problems. The jobs themselves have also changed over time and are as diverse as the products made, but in each case it is necessary for production and engineering teams to work closely together to achieve their targets efficiently and safely.

Profiles

Harvey Byrne, production manager, Ford Motor Company

Harvey Byrne, production manager of Ford's engine assembly plant, at Dagenham, is responsible for round-the-clock assembly of all the passenger and commercial vehicle engines produced by Ford in Britain — about 5000 every day.

Harvey graduated in metallurgy from Liverpool University in 1969.

'My intention had always been to go into production and on joining Ford I was placed at Dagenham as a production assistant. This gave me a general intro-duction into shop floor practices and systems. After three months I was made a production foreman on engine assembly, with 30 people working under me. It was my job to make sure that the cost, quality and quantity of output in my area met the objectives I'd been set.

'For the first time I became involved in shift work — strange at first, but I soon got used to it. Eighteen months later I became general foreman, which gave me greater responsibility, with four foremen and about a hundred hourly-paid employees reporting to me.

'After a course in production manage-ment, which included training in the skills of managing people, I was promoted to superintendent of the overhead camshaft assembly area. Here I was directly responsible to the production manager for the manufacture of 1000 engines a day and had two general foremen, seven foremen and 250 employees under my control.

'Having acted as superintendent in other machine areas to broaden my experience, I was appointed night shift manager of the Dagenham assembly plant which gave me total responsibility for some 2000 production employees plus related staff. All problems which couldn't be solved down the line were eventually channelled through to me.

whether direct production difficulties, service area problems or industrial relations problems.'

In early 1978 Harvey was appointed to his present post. Under him are five superintendents who are responsible for the assembly and testing of the engines of various models, and he begins each day with a meeting with them to review the previous day's performance and set priorities for the day ahead. They must ensure that the assembly lines meet the requirements of the other parts of the plant and, ultimately, the customer.

This requires careful planning of production schedules and assigning of tasks and targets to the various areas. At the same time they must keep a watchful eye on costs, quality and other matters such as safety. As Harvey has overall responsibility for all the people in the area, he must become involved in questions of discipline and industrial relations — in association with the personnel department — as these arise.

He liaises closely with other managers on the site and attends a production meeting every morning with his boss, the plant manager and the assistant plant

manager to look at the previous day's results and identify problems that may affect the day's production.

About the job Harvey has this to say:

'You have to accept in production that there are long hours, a lot of shift work involved and a good deal of frustration. It's a job where you have to put your hand to all types of problems but at the end of the day, having made a direct contribution to the efficiency and profitability of a firm, it gives you a satisfaction which outweighs all frustration.'

Albert Walsham, quality control supervisor, Ford Motor Company

Albert Walsham is supervisor of technical quality control at the Dagenham assembly plant, an extremely important function in the motor industry because of the safety aspects involved. Albert reports to the manager of quality control and his section is divided into three areas responsible for quality evaluation analysis, legal and safety surveillance and material inspection.

He graduated from Ford's own training school in 1962 with an ONC (Ordinary National Certificate) in mechanical engineering and held positions in all aspects of quality control until 1974 when he was made supervisor of a new department known as technical quality control.

'It is difficult to describe an average day as one of the best aspects of this job

is its variety and the unique nature of so many of the projects we undertake. However every job has some routine tasks.

'Each morning there is a quality meeting in the assembly plant attended by production management in the assembly and body plant areas. For this my department has to prepare a detailed analysis of product quality, highlighting problem areas. I then brief the managers before the meeting on the problems we have discovered, and steps are agreed on how to remedy them.

'Similarly each afternoon we have what is called a "uniform quality audit" where a selection of cars is checked, and points are awarded for defects. These points, totalled up, show us which sections have the greatest problems — paint, body, trim or whatever. Our reporting is done on a scoring system which is universal throughout Ford and so we can see clearly how our quality performance compares with other plants.

'These are the main routine tasks. In addition we prepare monthly and quarterly brochures on the plant's performance and conduct special studies as required. New systems and, on a much larger scale, new models pose a whole set of problems and decisions. We must advise on the best way of assessing quality and ironing out problems, and monitor the methods used in the plant to measure the quality of their production. Most important, it is our responsibility to liaise between the two shifts and ensure that an equal standard is maintained and the reporting is as fair and accurate as possible.

'Finally, our responsibility extends to contact with our suppliers to ensure that their supply of parts and raw materials meet the standards we require and have agreed with them.'

Bill Parker, factory engineer, Metal Box

Bill Parker is factory engineer at the Metal Box factory on the outskirts of Wisbech. He is responsible for the maintenance and repair of all the production machinery at the plant, which produces more than 1000 million cans a year for East Anglian tinned food manufacturers.

Bill likes to get to work a little before the 8.30am starting time so that he can have the day mapped out in his mind before the telephone starts ringing. Every day except Thursday starts with a round tour of the factory to discuss technical and management problems — 'and there are always some' — with the heads of his four departments.

On Thursdays he has his weekly technical meeting with his section heads, followed by the production meeting, chaired by the general manager. Present are Bill's boss, the manufacturing manager, the distribution and personnel managers, and Bill's counterparts on the production side. At this meeting they assess and plan for the demands that will be made on the factory in the coming week.

On other days Bill spends from 8.30 to 10am on his walkabout. His first call is on Melvin Brown, the machine repair department superintendent. This department employs some 60 people, with one foreman in charge on each shift. As its name suggests, it is responsible for keeping the production machinery in good running order — 17 can lines producing cans of sizes ranging from a small domestic pea tin to a one gallon catering pack; the 85-foot long ovens which bake protective laquer onto the inside of the tin plate which will be made into cans; the 16 power presses which make the can ends; and the lifting equipment, vacuum pumps and compressors.

Next he visits the electrical superintendent, Alex Henderson, whose three

shifts of electricians keep the lines supplied with power and the cans rolling. This is automatically controlled by electrical systems.

Bill's third head of department is the maintenance foreman in charge of work services, Henry Mainwaring. He has working for him a group of carpenters, bricklayers, boilermen and gardeners who help 'keep the factory a going concern'. They look after the entire plant area, all the essential services like water, heating, ventilation and the fabric of the buildings.

Finally he reaches the general stores where foreman Ron Ramsey supervises the supply of the factory's material requirements. The store holds solder, packaging and spare parts for all the machines on the site.

Satisfied that all his sections are running smoothly, Bill heads for the doors of his main 'customers' — the can lines. Here he makes sure that engineering is meeting the needs of production and discusses problems 'such as the supply of parts or a roof leak over a line'.

By 10 o'clock he is back in the office in time to tackle anything urgent from the morning's post before his visitors start arriving. Often these are specialists from the central group office of Metal Box, who have been called in to look at a specific problem. Others may be sales respresentatives from other firms, or members of his own sections with questions that could not be sorted out on his morning rounds, perhaps a matter relating to discipline or a foreman wanting to put men on overtime for a major job.

In the absence of visitors there are usually meetings in which he is involved followed by half an hour for lunch in the canteen. In the afternoon he repeats his tour of his section heads 'to keep in touch', then back to his office to deal with what remains of the post and routine administrative matters, many of which are concerned with meeting the requirements of government legislation.

Some of the queries he hands over to Roly Byster, his development engineer, who is involved in local development work for which it is not necessary to call in group specialists — for example small building projects and installation of new machinery.

'As you move further up the organisation more and more of your time is spent on matters not directly related to the technical side of engineering. But the challenge for which you are trained remains. Even though new developments, like installing a new type of laquer oven or converting to electronic control of production, may be masterminded elsewhere, when the parts are delivered the problem falls into our laps. It is up to us to assemble the package and get the machinery producing as quickly as possible.'

Carl Woods, toolmaker, Metal Box

Every other week Carl Woods' day starts early; he wakes at 5.15am to get ready to drive the eight miles from his house to the Metal Box factory for the 6 o'clock shift.

Carl left school at 16 and applied to Metal Box to do an engineering apprenticeship. He and seven others were selected from 150 applicants for the four-year scheme which trains skilled fitters, electricians and toolmakers. He spent his first two years in the training centre with one day a week at college learning basic engineering skills, followed by two years on the factory floor.

Carl works one week on day shift and the next on afternoons; there is a permanent night shift at the factory. He arrives, clocks in, changes into his overalls and grabs a cup of coffee on his way to the workshop. His main tasks are reconditioning of machine components, such as the press tools which punch out the ends of cans from sheets of tinplate; making custom-built tools when these are needed in the factory; and machining.

Checking the measurements on a press tool

His work must be extremely accurate. The parts are machined to tolerances of 0.003–0.0005 inches — less than half the thickness of a human hair — and errors result in their fitting together too tightly or too loosely so that the machine will not function properly.

Carl's boss is the foreman, who is in charge of a team of 14 skilled men, and is assisted by a chargehand. But because of the nature of his job, he doesn't need too much supervision. 'The foreman is too busy supervising work in progress on the factory floor', he says, 'so I can get on on my own.'

Carl breaks for brunch in the canteen from 10 to 10.30am and is then back on the job until the end of the shift at 2pm.

He has worked at Metal Box for seven years now — seven generally enjoyable years — 'but any job tends to get boring when you do the same thing day after day'. He could now go onto the factory floor as a fitter — 'a change of scene' — or perhaps move onto the training side for a while. He might be chosen for promotion to chargehand and later foreman. Alternatively he could move to a Metal Box factory in another part of the country, if a suitable vacancy arose, but he is not keen to leave his house and friends.

Class activity

Promotion in the machine shop — case study

You are the works manager of a large steel manufacturing company. Although your main responsibility is to see that production schedules are met and quality maintained, you find that much of your time is taken up with questions concerning the people who work in the factory. A typical example is your present dilemma: who should take the place of the machine shop superintendent who is due to retire next month? There are two possible candidates, both foremen under the superintendent.

George Childs, aged 57, is a first-class craftsman and highly respected throughout the firm, where he has worked for 20 years. He has already acted satisfactorily as machine shop superintendent when the superintendent has been on holiday. He left school at 15 and finds the paperwork involved with his job difficult, but copes adequately. You are sure George expects the promotion. In fact you overheard him telling one of his mates that he had promised his wife her own car when he got the job.

Alan Freeman, aged 29, is an ex-apprentice who won a scholarship to study for a degree in production engineering. He was made foreman five years ago. Since then George Childs has taken him under his wing and given advice freely from his much greater experience of the works. In return Alan has helped him with some of his paperwork. Since doing his degree he has been interested in the management side of the job and aims to be works manager himself one day. If he is to realise this ambition he must take a step up the ladder soon. He is convinced that the machine shop could be improved by bringing in modern methods which so far have been resisted by George and his boss.

Discussion

You realise that Alan Freeman has the potential to do well in the firm and that if not encouraged he may look elsewhere. The two foremen combine experience and technical knowledge and together make a first-class team. You would be very sorry to lose either of them. How would you tackle the problem?

Production versus engineering — case study

Ropework Limited, near Newcastle, produces steel ropes for industrial use; it supplies hoisting rope to local coal mines. The process is simple in principle — strands of steel wire are twisted many times to make a cable capable of supporting a lift cage full of men. The machines that do the twisting, however, are both vast and sophisticated, requiring careful maintenance, as faults in the rope could be a serious safety hazard. Maintenance is carried out on a monthly basis, but emergency repairs are made in between if necessary. These are avoided as far as possible because shutting down a machine means considerable loss of production and, therefore, money.

There are two men in charge of the Ropework plant: *Bob Woods*, production manager, and *Clive Jessop*, engineering manager, both of whom report to the managing director. Relations between them are not entirely amicable. Bob has been in the factory for years. He feels that production is all that matters, and everyone else should organise their work around his schedules. Clive is a highly qualified engineer. He knows that the machines will only operate efficiently if well looked after and feels that the production department sometimes leaves faults too long before getting repairs done, which results in far more work than should have been necessary.

Because of their different outlooks, the two men tend to avoid each other as much as possible.

The year 1979 has been a good one for Ropework. Threatened oil shortages and the cold winter have increased demand for coal and local industry has boomed. This month in particular orders are the largest

ever and Bob Woods realises that to shut down the plant for 24 hours for maintenance would prevent him meeting his production targets. He therefore sends a memo to Clive Jessop postponing the work for a fortnight.

Clive is furious. He thinks, 'Just let him wait till the breakdowns start. He won't get any extra help from us.'

One week later Dick Green, operator on number 4 line, notices that all is not well. One section of his 100-metre line seems to be overheating and, because he is an experienced operator, he can hear that the wire isn't running freely. He calls the engineering department to ask the machine repair foreman to get someone over right away.

What with one thing and another the repairs seem to take a long time that day, and by the time the machine is finally back in operation 48 hours of valuable production time have been lost, the production crew have had to work a weekend's overtime to catch up and the atmosphere on the shop floor is 'icy'.

Discussion

What went wrong and how could it be prevented from happening again?

Airborn Motors Limited — production simulation

You work in the manufacturing department of Airborn Motors Limited, which supplies passenger aircraft to countries all over the world. At the moment you have five main customers whose aircraft are distinguishable by the marks on their wings.

The aim of this exercise is for groups of six students to simulate aircraft manufacture in the factory. To do so they will need to organise their production schedules and use of labour, order raw materials and practise their own quality control. They will then be assessed on the efficiency of their production.

The exercise simulates one year's manufacture.

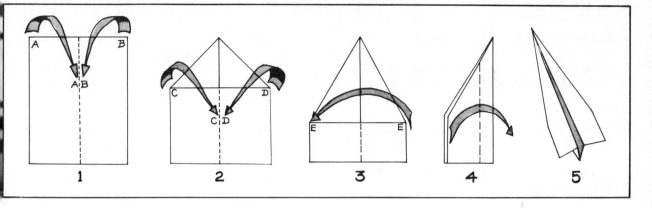

Products and design

The aircraft are constructed following the pattern shown in the figure above. The range of products made by the company is shown in the table below.

Product Range

Customer	Size (cm)	Markings	
A	29.50	Red	□
A	20.75	Red	□
B	29.50	Blue	□
B	20.75	Blue	□
C	29.50	Red	△
C	20.75	Red	△
D	29.50	Blue	△
D	20.75	Blue	△
E	29.50	None	
E	20.75	None	

The size is measured from the tip of the nose to the tail, and the markings are either 1 cm squares or 1 cm equilateral triangles.

Sales orders

The marketing department has informed you that your total order for the year is shown in the table below.

Sales Orders for the Year

Customer	Order	
	Large plane	Small plane
A	16	10
B	20	10
C	10	20
D	20	5
E	15	25

Raw materials

These are kept by the teacher and consist of

White   A4 paper
Red   A4 paper
Blue   A4 paper

White paper can only be ordered in batches of 30 sheets. Coloured sheets can be ordered singly. The orders must be put through in writing and be dealt with in order of arrival. There may be a delay between ordering and receiving the materials.

Equipment

Each group is provided with manufacturing equipment which consists of

1 pair of scissors
2 sticks of paper glue
2 pencils
2 rulers

Organisation of work and production method

You are left to decide how you will carry out the work and how it should be planned. Areas to consider are

- Production planning
- Stock control
- Supervision
- Organisation of labour
- Quality control.

You have 30 minutes to complete the manufacturing target, including planning the work.

Quality control

Your industry is one in which safety is a major factor and quality control therefore very important. No aeroplane may be sold if damaged or not to specifications (for example, if the wings are obviously different in size and the markings poorly made).

Finished planes are required to pass a minimum flight test of five metres. It is not necessary to test every plane, but spot checks will be carried out by the teacher at the end of the production period.

Assessment

Points will be awarded to groups along the following lines.

> 2 points for each large aircraft completed
> 1 point for each small aircraft completed
> 10 points in addition for each customer's whole order completed

Less

> 4 points for each aircraft which has to be rejected during the exercise

8 points for any aircraft rejected by the teacher
1 point for every 10 sheets of white paper left unused
1 point for every single sheet of coloured paper left unused.

Discussion

After assessing the groups consider the following questions:

(1) Which group was the most successful in terms of points? What were the reasons for this?
(2) What methods of organisation of the workforce seemed the most effective? What were the reasons for this?
(3) Was the most efficient group also the most enjoyable one in which to work?
(4) What lessons can you learn from this exercise that would apply to manufacturing in a real factory?

Finance

4

Outline of the function

Companies, like the rest of us, must keep a close check on their finances, and most have a separate department whose special responsibility this is. The finance department monitors *when* money is coming in and going out; *where* it is coming from and going to; and *how much* is flowing backwards and forwards.

The financial manager must have at his finger tips the exact position of the company at any moment and the information that management needs to make decisions on matters such as investment, expansion and diversification. His staff must be able to advise on questions such as 'should we spend £1m on modernising our old factory or £8m on building a new one?', 'is it worth investing £1000 on a new machine which will save only 1p per item manufactured?' and 'how long would it take for this machine to pay for itself?'

Finding the right answers to these sorts of questions could make the difference between a profit and a loss.

The financial manager also has advisers outside

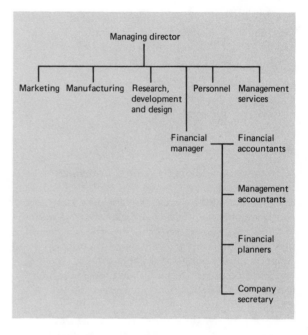

the company — mainly the company's bank manager, stockbrokers, and auditors — whom he will meet regularly to review financial performance.

The staff of the finance department of most large firms is fairly small, but highly qualified, and consists of chartered accountants, cost and management accountants, financial analysts, accounts clerks and bookkeepers. Their work falls under these general headings.

Financial accounting

The department prepares regular financial accounts on the company's operations, usually monthly, together with the full annual accounts which the law requires. The main accounting elements are

- Balance sheets
- Profit and loss accounts
- Cash flow forecasts.

Management accounting

In order to keep a close check on the running of the business management needs more detailed information than that provided by these basic financial statements. Management accountants co-ordinate the preparation of budgets by managers in other departments, translate these into cash terms and combine them into an overall annual company budget. They then monitor the performance against the budget and provide regular feedback to the departments concerned and the managing director.

To be effective the management accounts staff must work closely with line management, providing them with a helpful service. A budget for the manufacturing department is not likely to work if it is dreamt up by someone sitting in a carpeted office on the other side of the works, with no idea of the problems in keeping to it. The management accountant's chief responsibility is to see that line management and supervisors are kept informed of their sections' performance so that they can sort out any problems before too much damage is done.

Management accountants may also review proposals on price, and establish how much money is available for sales campaigns and advertising. In this area they work closely with marketing.

Financial planning

Companies must be continually looking ahead and the planners look at the financial aspects of future company plans, whether they be short-term plans on purchase of equipment or the feasibility of new projects or products, or major long-term strategies on mergers or expansions.

Tax and auditing

In addition large companies employ specialists to deal with areas such as taxation and auditing. Company taxation is an extremely complex subject and experts are needed to see that a business can minimise its tax bill without being guilty of tax evasion.

Legal and secretarial work

One position which requires special mention and in a large company may justify a separate department is that of the company secretary. He deals with the firm's legal obligations, particularly as regards the Companies Act, and often other matters such as property contracts and patents. The increasing amounts of legislation affecting companies have led to an expansion of the role of this department, but firms often use outside legal advisers for this type of work.

The company secretary in a small company may also be called on to look after the administration of office staff, the telephone switchboard, the stores and other areas which in a larger firm would fall under specialised departments.

From this description you can see that the finance department is by no means divorced from the rest of the company, but is an essential and integral part of it. The financial manager is a key figure on the management team. The role of those who work in finance is essentially one of 'advising' rather than 'deciding', but in today's fiercely competitive industrial worls their influence is considerable.

Profiles

Alan Stewart, accountant, Mars

Alan Stewart is quite new to Mars, having joined the company only last year to work as an accountant in the financial accounting division.

'Before this I was a chartered accountant with a firm of professional accountants, providing an accounting service to outside customers.

'It took me three years to qualify, including both the exams and gaining necessary practical experience in a firm of chartered accountants, but I found this type of work rather sterile and decided to turn my attention to opportunities in industry.

'The problem with professional accountancy is that it is very difficult to become involved with the firms whose accounting systems one is monitoring. Recommendations one makes for change are not necessarily implemented. The reverse is true if one is part of the financial division of a particular firm. Here at Mars I do have an influence on the review of various systems and I can feel myself committed to the aims of the company as a whole.'

What about the job itself?

'I am responsible for the whole of what is called the bought ledger department. This deals with control of all raw material and packaging costs, so that I work closely with the commodity buyers.

'I have 10 people working for me and I report to the financial accountant, who, in addition to my area, controls the payroll department and the accountants who keep a check on overhead costs such as electricity and rent.

'The department works on four-week cycles and the first two weeks each time are taken up with the preparation of accounts. Once the figures have been produced I look at any differences between the actual costs incurred and those which were forecast. I have to discover the reasons for these cost variances and write reports discussing these reasons and suggesting improvements.

'As well as this I spend time reviewing existing systems and recommending new, improved methods for accounting and cost control. Also through the tight control of cost variances for raw material and packaging I am involved in predicting the future prices of these commodities.

'The work brings me into contact with many departments at Mars and gives me a chance to effect real improvements within the organisation and to see the results of these changes. Which brings me back to my reasons for choosing a career in industry; greater involvement and greater job satisfaction.'

Sandra Garrett, bought ledger supervisor, Mars

Sandra Garrett is bought ledger supervisor in Alan Stewart's department at Mars.

'I joined the company 10 years ago as a trainee, which meant that I spent my first two years working in different departments to get as much experience as possible and to see how the whole organisation fits together, while going to a technical college one day a week to complete my training.

'Since then I have been employed in various parts of the finance department — as a costing clerk, then an accounts clerk and now as bought ledger supervisor, working directly for the accountants.'

The Mars finance department consists of about 50 people, most of whom work in a large open plan office in the Dundee Road Plant on the Slough Trading Estate. Sandra's job involves supervising the payment of invoices for things that the company has purchased. These include

raw materials, packaging and finished goods.

She, like Alan, works on a four-week cycle.

'I spend the first two weeks of a period helping to prepare the monthly accounts, which are published in the second week and distributed to all departments in the company. These accounts cover all aspects of Mars's performance over the preceding period and I am involved in calculating the productivity of various departments, their use of raw materials and sales volumes.

'I also help with what are called finished goods reconciliations which ensure that we can trace the whereabouts of all goods produced by the factory. Finally I use all this information, which I have collected from other departments, such as manufacturing and sales, collated and standardised, to update the profit and loss account.

'During the second half of the accounting period my work is of a more general kind and its nature depends on which projects are in hand in the department. As problems arise I am asked to produce the relevant figures or to help clarify the points in question. This could be work on insurance declarations or sales accounts, or it may simply involve answering queries.

'While most of my work tends to revolve around figures the specific tasks are very varied and, particularly during the second half of the period they never become dull, routine or repetitive. It is

quite easy to move jobs within the finance department, so that, too, gives plenty of scope for change.

'One thing I've learnt from working in finance, figures aren't boring.'

Richard Beattie, co-ordinator sales profit and budget analysis, Ford of Europe

Since graduating in business studies in 1976 Richard Beattie has filled three positions in the Ford Finance department. This is part of what is called Ford of Europe, a central organisation, based in Essex, which co-ordinates long-term planning for Ford's operations throughout Europe.

'I spent just under 18 months in administrative overhead and manpower analysis, six months in profit analysis and I have recently moved to the section which deals with sales profit and budget analysis.

'The administrative and commercial expense budget for Ford's European operations is currently in the region of $200m which is mainly made up of the payment of salaries. My first job had two major functions. The first was to review in detail the annual budget requirements submitted to the finance department by other departments on both the manufacturing and non-manufacturing sides, and to recommend to management possible areas of expense reduction and

corresponding profit improvement.

'The second function was to monitor the income statement of Ford of Europe Incorporated and to ensure that expense incurred ($100m in 1976) was charged out to its affiliates, the national companies in Europe. This proved to be of

particular interest to me as it required constant liaison with Ford's legal departments in order to minimise the complex taxation and exchange control problems that can occur throughout Europe and the United States.

'My second job, as sales revenue analyst in the profit analysis section, involved forecasting on a monthly basis total revenues from the sale of vehicles, parts, engines and transmissions in both the domestic and export markets. This data was then submitted to Ford U.S. for consolidation in company-wide profit data, together with the effect on revenue of decisions on prices and the amounts spent on such things as advertising and sales promotion.

'My current position deals with co-ordinating the preparation of the 15 national sales companies' annual budgets and developing their short-range business plans. This job has the added attraction that it enables me to travel to Europe in order to keep in touch with our affiliates there.'

Richard Tilt, financial analyst, Ford of Europe

As a financial analyst in the product development group of Ford of Europe, Richard Tilt's job is to review the implications of proposed product engineering changes that require capital expenditure and to present detailed assessments of these changes for consideration by senior management.

'The review process starts with the issue of an engineering problem report and change request forms outlining the product problem and the proposed remedial action. It ends with the release of funds needed to implement the change.

'The request might be for $150 for a new exhaust emission decal legally required for Fiestas to be sold in

California, or for $500 000 to replace a roof-panel-mounted, interior driving mirror with one that is fixed to the windscreen.

'Although the financial analysis is relatively straightforward and much the same for each proposal, it is the products and the techniques used to find, analyse and interpret all the relevant data that make the job interesting.

'There was no choice but to spend $150 for the decal, but does it really cost $500 000 to change the mirror? Is a major rearrangement of the assembly line really necessary; what are the alternatives . . . have they been fully evaluated; is the manufacturing group adopting the optimum route in terms of

investment; is it a good business decision to implement the change?

'These are the kind of questions I ask and have to find answers for. It makes my job demanding and never boring. Each day there are new problems to tackle, frequently with a time limit in which to identify and resolve the issues and make a recommendation. And all the time I must maintain close liaison with European colleagues in other parts of the business!'

Class activity

Avoca Dopear Limited — case study*

Avoca Dopear Limited produces ball-point pens. Its sales and profits have for many years been rising steadily, but recently have levelled off at approximately £1m and £100 000 respectively. Market research indicates that the felt-tip pen is taking an increasing share of the market and the management of Avoca Dopear has decided that it must enter this field. The most recently produced balance sheet reveals the following figures:

Balance sheet

	£			£
Capital	300 000	Fixed assets		
Reserves	250 000	(factory)		300 000
Creditors	100 000	(machinery)		70 000
		Stock		150 000
		Debtors		120 000
		Bank		10 000
	650 000			650 000

The company owns a 60-acre site, the existing factory covering 20 acres, 15 acres being devoted to parking and recreational facilities and the remainder being waste ground. There is a proposal to erect an extension to the premises on part of the waste ground to house machinery for producing the felt-tip pens. Planning permission has been obtained and the costs of building are reckoned to be £200 000; this estimate includes all professional fees.

The new machinery will cost a further £50 000, and the additional stockholdings required are expected to be about another £50 000. About £20 000 of wages and overheads will have to be covered before proceeds from sales of the new product begin to cover production costs. A further £40 000 is earmarked to promote the new product and £10 000 to cover the expected increase in debtors.

* This case study was prepared by Lloyds Bank Limited.

The company thus requires:

£	
200 000	Factory
50 000	Machinery
40 000	Promotional costs
20 000	Wages/overheads
50 000	Extra stock
10 000	Extra debtors
370 000	

In addition it is decided that a further £30 000 should be raised as a contingency to cover increasing costs as sales of the new product escalate.

Possible sources of finance

A company wishing to raise money has a number of different possible sources to consider, the choice depending largely on the use to which the funds are to be put.

Working capital has been traditionally raised from banks, and the loan is reviewed annually. Provided that the company is running satisfactorily, the bank will not insist on repayment.

The money to pay for fixed assets, such as a factory and machinery, may be raised by issuing shares or fixed interest loans through the Stock Exchange. Loans can also be sought from banks and organisations like Finance for Industry (FFI), which makes long-term funds available to small businesses.

When considering how best to go about raising funds management of the company must assess its future prospects, its ability to attract people to invest their savings by buying shares in the company, or to repay the loan. Prospective lenders will also want to be satisfied that the company can offer security for the loan.

The company must be able to offer the prospect of competitive dividend payment to its shareholders, and to 'service' the loan (the interest charges and repayments) out of its profits. The interest rate charged by the clearing banks is influenced by the minimum lending rate which is set by the Bank of England. For long-term loans the rate is reviewed from time to time in the light of current market conditions. The rate will normally be higher than that quoted for a short-term loan from a clearing bank.

Sales forecast

Sales in the old product are expected to fall. The company considers that over the next five years they will drop to one-half of the present volume and then level off.

The market for the new product may be difficult to break into as other firms have already begun production. Company management considers that the market for felt-tip pens will grow rapidly and that they will be able to capture an increasing share of it using their existing outlets for ball-point pens. They must, however, calculate what level of sales is required to break even, that is the point at which sales revenue equals the costs of production. If this level of sales cannot be reached initially, then further finance is required to cover the production losses.

Management's decision

The company decides to negotiate an overdraft facility of £100 000 with its clearing bank. This could be reduced by £25 000 per annum from profits generated by the new product so as to be repaid completely during four years.

The remaining £300 000 is to be raised as a long-term loan, repayable over 20 years, from a merchant bank or an organisation such as ICFC, part of FFI.

Discussion

Consider the following questions.

(1) Is management's decision on how to raise the money the best one in the circumstances?
(2) Is the company likely to receive this financial support?
(3) Is there any way the company could reduce its borrowing requirement?
(4) Would there be any side effects of the scheme for the local area?

The CLS Company -- working capital control exercise*

Introduction

This exercise is intended to illustrate the following points:

- The need in business to consider the cash implications of a decision as well as the impact on profit
- The effect of variations from expectations which could occur once the company is in operation
- The relationship between profit and cash and the compilation of a set of accounts.

In the exercise you are asked to produce cash flow forecasts for three situations in which the company finds itself and to prepare a profit and loss account and balance sheet.

Background information

You, the syndicate, have evolved a new product and decide to invest money in a company to manufacture and sell it. You can raise £150 000 in cash and need to spend £25 000 on plant before you can start production. You estimate that each month you need £40 000 for wages and salaries; £5000 for expenses and £40 000 for materials.

It takes two weeks to produce the finished product and you have negotiated some initial contracts to take up all your production for £100 000 per month. Your suppliers will give you two months' credit and your customers expect the same.

For the purposes of the exercises

- Ignore taxation, interest (unless otherwise stated) and depreciation.
- Assume all months to be equal in length.
- Use month 0 (see the worksheet on the next page) for recording any cash spent before work commences at 0800 on the first Monday of month 1.
- There is no credit on plant or expenses.
- The work sheets are based on a 10-month period to indicate the continuing nature of the business. The period is not significant.

Exercise 1

First fill in a work sheet such as that on the next page for the cash flow budget of the company. Consider the implications of this and discuss the following questions:

* This case study was prepared by Brian Wood, financial controller of BOC Limited.

Work Sheet		Cash Flow Budget										£ thousand
	Months											
	0	1	2	3	4	5	6	7	8	9	10	
Inflows Cash at start of month												
Add Cash received from customers												
A. Total Inflow												
Outflows Plant Wages and salaries Expenses Materials												
B. Total Outflow												
Cash at end of Month (A − B)												
Carry forward to start of next month												

Cash flow sheet for the CLS Company

(1) Is the business profitable?
(2) Will you have sufficient cash?
(3) If not, will you need assistance?
(4) If so, how much, when and for how long?

Now prepare a profit and loss account for the 10 months and a balance sheet to show the position of the CLS company at the end of the period. Discuss the significance of these financial statements. You might compare them with the published accounts of real companies which are printed in several newspapers or are available from the companies themselves.

Exercise 2

Suppose that one of your customers, who takes half your second month's output, fails to pay.

(1) Fill in a second cash flow forecast like that above to show the effect of this and discuss its implications for the company.
(2) What steps could you as management have taken to see that this type of problem did not occur?
(3) What action should you take now that it has?

Exercise 3

After five months, business at the CLS company is going very well, orders are coming in fast and the enquiry rate is rising rapidly. You find that you could double the existing production. Fill in a third work sheet to illustrate this situation, assuming production is doubled in month 6 and onwards. (Assume for this exercise that the problem in Exercise 2 did not take place).

(1) What is the effect on cash flow of doubling production?
(2) Could you afford it?
(3) What should you do?
(4) Should you wait for a while? If so, when should you act?

Some common terms and phrases -- finance

Assets What the company owns. *Fixed assets* are items such as plant, machinery and buildings and *current assets* are stock, money owed to the company and cash.

Balance sheet Shows the financial position of the company at a specific time. On one side of the page is the value of all its assets and on the other its liabilities. See the figure on page 36.

Budget Financial plan or target.

Balance sheet-what we own and what we owe

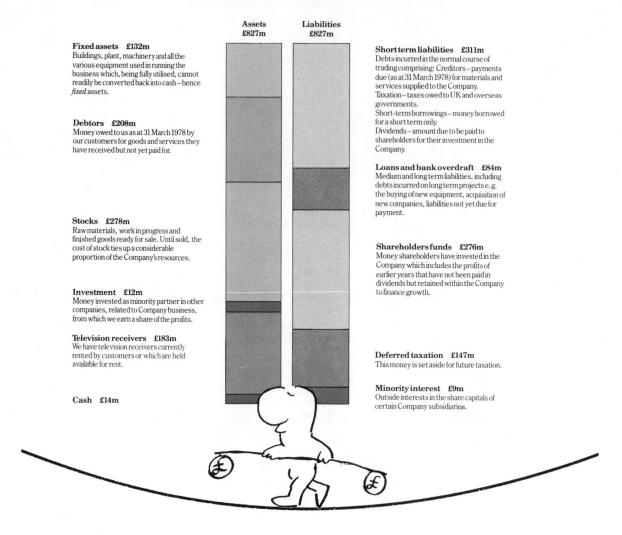

Fixed assets £132m
Buildings, plant, machinery and all the various equipment used in running the business which, being fully utilised, cannot readily be converted back into cash – hence *fixed* assets.

Debtors £208m
Money owed to us as at 31 March 1978 by our customers for goods and services they have received but not yet paid for.

Stocks £278m
Raw materials, work in progress and finished goods ready for sale. Until sold, the cost of stock ties up a considerable proportion of the Company's resources.

Investment £12m
Money invested as minority partner in other companies, related to Company business, from which we earn a share of the profits.

Television receivers £183m
We have television receivers currently rented by customers or which are held available for rent.

Cash £14m

Assets £827m

Liabilities £827m

Short term liabilities £311m
Debts incurred in the normal course of trading comprising: Creditors – payments due (as at 31 March 1978) for materials and services supplied to the Company.
Taxation – taxes owed to UK and overseas governments.
Short-term borrowings – money borrowed for a short term only.
Dividends – amount due to be paid to shareholders for their investment in the Company.

Loans and bank overdraft £84m
Medium and long term liabilities, including debts incurred on long term projects e.g. the buying of new equipment, acquisition of new companies, liabilities not yet due for payment.

Shareholders funds £276m
Money shareholders have invested in the Company which includes the profits of earlier years that have not been paid in dividends but retained within the Company to finance growth.

Deferred taxation £147m
This money is set aside for future taxation.

Minority interest £9m
Outside interests in the share capitals of certain Company subsidiaries.

(a) Thorn's balance sheet as at 31 March 1978 as it was explained to the employees
Source: Thorn Electrical Industries Ltd special report for employees

Cash flow forecast Shows when money is expected to come in or go out over a period (usually 12 months), where it is coming from and on what it will be spent.

Contribution Selling price of goods minus the direct cost of their manufacture.

Creditors Companies and people to whom the business owes money.

Debtors Companies and people who owe money to the business.

Depreciation Spreading the cost of a fixed asset, such as buildings or equipment, over its working life.

Direct costs Costs, such as labour costs and the cost of materials, which vary according to the number of items manufactured. Also called *variable costs*.

Equity The owners' claims against the business, sometimes called *shareholders' funds*. This is regarded as a liability because it belongs not to the business but to its shareholders.

Profit and loss account-our income and what we do with it

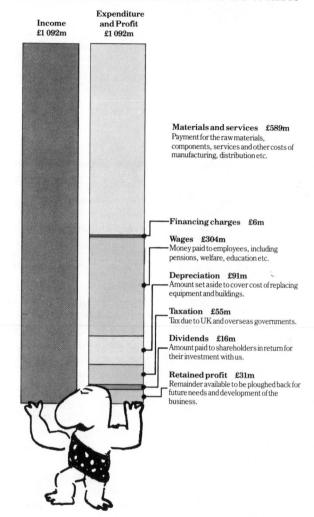

Income
£1 092m

Expenditure
and Profit
£1 092m

Income from home and overseas after
eliminating sales within divisions.

Materials and services   £589m
Payment for the raw materials,
components, services and other costs of
manufacturing, distribution etc.

Financing charges   £6m

Wages   £304m
Money paid to employees, including
pensions, welfare, education etc.

Depreciation   £91m
Amount set aside to cover cost of replacing
equipment and buildings.

Taxation   £55m
Tax due to UK and overseas governments.

Dividends   £16m
Amount paid to shareholders in return for
their investment with us.

Retained profit   £31m
Remainder available to be ploughed back for
future needs and development of the
business.

(b) Thorn's profit and loss account for the twelve months ended 31 March 1978

Gearing   The ratio of the company's borrowings to
the equity.

Indirect costs   Costs which do not vary according to
the volume of production, also called *fixed costs* or
overheads.

Liabilities   The claims against the business, such as
equity and loans from the bank. Overdrafts, dividend
payments and money owed to creditors all referred to
as *current liabilities.*

Profit and loss account   A statement of sales, costs,
expenses and profit over a period of time (usually
12 months). This is also known as an income statement.
See figure above.

Stock   Inventory of goods on hand, including stores,
raw materials, work in progress and finished goods.

Working capital   Current assets less current liabilities,
which represents the capital used in the day-to-day
running of the business.

Personnel

5

Outline of the function

Personnel management is concerned with selecting the people who work in an organisation and developing them into an effective, trained workforce so that they can make their best contribution to its success, both as individuals and as members of a team.

In a small company there may be only one person responsible for all the varied aspects of personnel work, but most large firms employ a number of specialists who form a structured personnel department. There is usually a personnel manager, or director, responsible to the board, who has under him middle managers responsible for the department's main functions. These are the following.

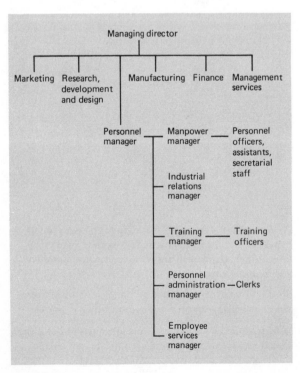

Selection and recruitment

This section recruits new employees as vacancies arise, in association with line management. Its staff advertise vacancies, deal with applications, hold interviews, and make sure new employees settle into their jobs.

Training and development

The training section is concerned with giving people the skills to do their jobs efficiently and helping them develop their careers. Its staff are responsible for organising apprentice schemes, providing specialised training courses for employees, such as selling staff and office staff, and training and developing managers and supervisors. With the recent emphasis in every industry on the importance of managing people and the realisation that every supervisor does not have to be a 'born leader', this management development function has become increasingly important. The section is also often involved in re-training employees to take up new jobs within the company; this is particularly important in industries in which new technology has led to changes in the skills required. In the biggest companies, training staff will probably

Employee services

Traditionally, personnel managers were primarily concerned with employees' welfare. Today this has been largely replaced by the idea of employee services, of which the two main ones deal with health and safety. Personnel staff are still concerned with the welfare of employees when outside the company but this aspect is increasingly becoming the responsibility of local authority social workers.

Manpower planning

The personnel department must see that the right people are available to fill the right jobs at the right time, even though the firm's manpower requirements may vary considerably over a period of years. Forecasting these needs and reviewing the workforce and its development will help assure that these requirements are met.

Salary administration

The personnel department is responsible for ensuring that salaries and other conditions of employment are appropriate. They may also deal with the administration of paying wages. Records of people employed by the firm will be kept by personnel clerks. This is an important area because there is a statutory requirement for companies to have on hand detailed information about their workforces and to be able to supply this on request.

From this list you can see that personnel management is not directly concerned with managing people, except for those who work within the department itself. Personnel management in fact forms a part of every manager's and supervisor's job, but the personnel department provides specialist knowledge and services to help line managers to make the most effective use of the human resources of the organisation.

run all or most of these courses themselves, while other firms often make use of outside training facilities such as local colleges.

Industrial relations

This is one of the major functions of the personnel department. It covers negotiations with trade unions and all areas of communication within the firm between employees and their employer. In this area more, perhaps, than any other the personnel officer is a highly skilled specialist, well versed in aspects such as the relevant legislation, providing an advisory service to line management on whose shoulders responsibility for employee relations ultimately rests.

Profiles

Warren Bradley, personnel manager, Tower Housewares

Pots, pans and people make up the working day of Warren Bradley. He is the personnel manager of Tower Housewares, which manufactures the familiar Tower saucepans, frying pans, pressure cookers and electric slow cookers.

Based in Wolverhampton, the company employs 630 people. As personnel manager Warren reports to the managing director, and has a personnel officer to assist him with day-to-day personnel

matters. He is also responsible for the canteens and for round-the-clock security cover for the factory.

'My role is as adviser to all the other managers in the business, and the board of directors, on matters like recruitment, training, safety and a host of others which come under the heading of human relations. It is essentially a practical role which reaches into all

the other activities in the organisation. Its central purpose is the development and effective use of people.

'I am responsible for seeing that the selection process matches the right people to vacant jobs – through interviews and, sometimes, carefully chosen tests.

'I must ensure that the special skills and knowledge enabling all our employees to carry out their work effectively is provided, either through external courses, or coaching and tuition in our own training unit. Employees who perform well have to be identified by their managers so that they can be developed and promoted into bigger jobs. The personnel manager must provide the systems needed for this to happen, and in this way the company keeps its good staff as they acquire new skills to apply at more senior levels.'

The personnel department also organises specialised training courses. For example, one was recently held on finance to help those who must know about the essential part money and cost control plays in the success of the business. This is particularly important for supervisors who often have had no financial training but are responsible for budgets in their sections.

Warren sees one of his key functions as 'to be continually looking for ways of improving working relationships in the organisation by promoting consultation, discussion and understanding about company performance and important decisions that are being taken'.

As part of this role he acts as secretary to the newly-formed Company Council at which 20 representatives of the different departments meet two of the directors quarterly to discuss matters of mutual interest, such as sales forecasts, product development and company performance.

He also sits as a management representative, with the works manager and manufacturing director, on a Joint Productivity Committee which includes

Warren Bradley and Laraine Malvern checking the safety guarding on a lid-notching machine

the 13 shop stewards in the factory and staff representatives. At these meetings matters relating to production and subjects of particular concern to the shop floor are discussed. 'These meetings help to develop good relationships between management and shop stewards and representatives on which the company places considerable emphasis', he says.

In addition he arranges a quarterly meeting of all the managers and supervisors to talk about company results, sales forecasts and so on, and represents

Tower management in pay negotiations with the four unions on the site.

All in all, a job with plenty of variety. Warren Bradley is a graduate of Aston University, but he emphasises that the qualifications for success in personnel work need not be through formal exams. 'An interest in people, an ability to communicate and listen to arguments are far more important', he says. 'People expect to be treated reasonably well at work – after all, it is a major part of their lives. It is my responsibility to see that this happens.'

Laraine Malvern, personnel officer, Tower Housewares

Laraine Malvern is personnel officer at Tower Housewares. With her staff of three she is responsible for providing a personnel service for the company's 450 hourly and weekly-paid employees.

'One of my main activities is recruitment and training. When managers find they need additional staff, or to replace someone who is leaving, I have to decide how best to find them – through a Job Centre, an employment agency, a newspaper or local radio advertisement, or maybe by promoting within the company. Once application forms have been completed, promising applicants are invited for interview. These may be

held by myself or my assistant, probably with a manager or supervisor interviewing with us.

'When new employees start work, on the first day we carry out what is called 'induction' training. We introduce them to the company using slides and other visual aids to give some idea of the size and type of organisation they will be working for. We explain the various functions and procedures which are peculiar to our company, such as pension rights, sick pay schemes, holidays, disciplinary procedures, health and safety at work, and so on.

'Once the employee is taken into the department I am responsible for monitoring any further training he or she is given, either inside or outside the company.'

Laraine's unit also keeps accurate records for each person at Tower – 'an important function as many other departments rely on us to produce statistics on the number of people employed, the types of job they do, wages information, age and training, among others.'

'We are concerned with an employee's welfare at work. I have a surgery attached to the unit staffed by a full-time nurse who deals with most minor accidents and illnesses. We have a doctor who visits the factory once a week to advise on any more severe occupational health problems. Another of my staff runs a company shop for employees to buy Tower products.

'A responsibility closely linked to welfare is that of safety on the site. This is a part of the job which has developed considerably with the recent legislation. I liaise with our maintenance engineer and departmental managers to try to ensure that all machinery and equipment used in the factory is safe, and that all jobs are done in the safest possible environment. Each department has its own safety representative and inspections are carried out on a regular basis. I write up a safety report after every inspection and investigate any accidents which do occur, preparing reports for the insurance company and the factory inspector.

'Employment has also become subject to an increasing amount of legislation in the last few years, covering such areas as unfair dismissal, sex discrimination, maternity leave and time off for trade union activities, and I am responsible for advising supervisors and managers on its interpretation and implementation.'

Laraine does not find it easy to describe a typical personnel officer's job because so little of it is routine work.

'One day can be wholly taken up with safety matters, whilst another may be spent on training and the next day I may be interviewing from nine until five. But essentially I am concerned with people and with providing Tower House-wares with an effective workforce — without which there would be no housewares.'

The role of the personnel department

The role of the personnel department as an advisory one cannot be overemphasised. This is how Peter Linklater, the personnel director of Shell U.K., sees the personnel management function.

The line manager's best friend
Peter Linklater

The personnel function, with its authority stemming from the chief executive, is concerned with two distinct sets of policies and their implementation: they are employment policies and deployment policies. Employment policies deal essentially with remuneration and other terms and conditions of employment. They are largely environmental, being determined by market forces, and it is of prime importance that they be unambiguous and easily ascertained. Their implementation can and should be left to line management. Good employment policies do not in themselves generate profit nor do they motivate people to work more effectively. Badly conceived or communicated employment policies act as potent dissatisfiers. They have more potential for negative harm than positive good.

Direct involvement
Deployment policies are designed to achieve the objective of having the right people in the right numbers with the right experience in the right place at the right time. Success in these policies spells the difference between profit and loss, survival and extinction. It is arguable that these represent the most important contribution of the personnel function to the achievement of business goals. They encompass recruitment, training, organisation development and management selection. Bad employee relations are much more likely to stem from poor managers than from poor employment policies.

It has been something of a tradition in the U.K. for line managers to leave all aspects of employment policies, i.e. employee relations, to the personnel department. Line managers do not like 'arguing' with shop stewards, staff committees or even their own work groups. People are much more intractable than products or machinery. On the other hand line managers are convinced that they alone should make the recruitment selection, decide who is promoted and how many people they need to do the job. To give an example: we constructed a new refinery on Teesport. Having established the technology, the first thing was to identify the five best shift foremen and send them (some had previously been shop stewards) to our most recently organised refineries in the U.S. and Canada to make sure they had a full understanding of the latest ways of operating in a totally flexible, capital-intensive refinery. We had an operating superintendent who was the boss of the shift managers (this was a refinery with a capital investment of £10–12m and for 18 hours out of 24 is run by a shift manager).

The superintendent, with the shift manager, organised the work system — the way in which they would recruit, train and so forth — and we, very deliberately, gave them a personnel adviser. A framework of employment policies was provided. So far as the deployment side was concerned staffing, management, total framework and organisation would be handled with head office advice. Line management got on with it and the system worked extremely well, and still does. Every new line manager coming into this type of situation has the same first reaction. 'Do I really have to talk to the shop steward and have to negotiate with the local union official? I have been brought up to believe that the labour manager does that.'

In fact line managers are much better at contributing to, and implementing, employment policies than they think they are (or they are failing in one of their prime tasks of leadership) — and not as good as they think they are in the area of deployment policies where positive integration with overall corporate planning objectives is essential.

The personnel function is, therefore, the friend of middle management even though it may appear to take decision-taking from middle management in the deployment area — because it sees more of the game on the chief executives' behalf; this is its area of maximum contribution to the motivation of people and maintenance of business effectiveness.

Participation

Another cognate area of great importance in the relationship between middle managers and the personnel function is employee participation, or 'industrial democracy'. Employees should have the opportunity of influencing decisions that bear directly on their work environment and employment prospects.

For top management to reach the best decisions it needs to have a good idea of a broad cross-section of opinion, including minority views. A manager wants to give weight to the views of his employees before taking actions for which he has the ultimate personal responsibility — or before he contributes to the formulation of policy decisions to which he will be committed.

Indeed the personnel function should be the good line manager's best friend, providing a clear framework of employment policies and well-trained colleagues. It is worth reading Peter Drucker's list of the seven areas in which sustained performance is vital to corporate success — failure in any one will vitiate all the others.

(1) Innovation
(2) Employee attitude and performance
(3) Management selection and development
(4) Productivity
(5) Public reputation
(6) Market standing
(7) Access to finance.

These points are the key to achievement. The first five relate directly to effective performance by the personnel function as the alter ego of the chief executive. Perhaps only the first requires elaboration. Any company that ceases to innovate will die yet there are major industries where the high standards of competitive research produce a stalemate in technology or product — the oil industry? — yet innovation in social policies and the more effective deployment of human resources is essential or creeping paralysis will seize the organisation.

Source: Industrial Society, September/October 1977.

Class activity

Bryanston Enterprises Limited — role play

The following role play shows the different areas in which the personnel department may become involved, and the way that not everyone in a company is always in agreement on where priorities lie.

Background information

Situated near Watford, Bryanston Enterprises Limited manufactures a range of piping for use in plumbing and

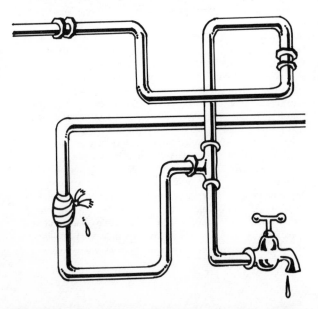

heating. It employs some 700 people — 600 in the factory and 100 at head office which is on the same site.

Bryanston is a long-established company and is still in its original somewhat antiquated premises, largely because the managing director is not keen on what he calls 'change for change's sake' — particularly when it involves spending money. The firm has no official personnel policies (or any other written policies for that matter), no proper communication or consultative machinery, no incentive payment scheme or suggestion scheme for employees. It has also never placed much emphasis on training: instead it has always taken the view that time spent 'off the job' was non-productive time.

Bryanston's personnel director has been concerned for some time about these problems and has managed to persuade the managing director to allow him to propose some priorities for the personnel department to be discussed when they meet next week. He has, therefore, called a 30-minute meeting with the personnel manager and his three senior staff to agree on the key areas of the department's activities and draw up a list of points for action over the next six months.

Act out the role play. Either use one cast with the rest of the class watching or have several different groups meet at the same time and all come together for discussion at the end.

The characters

Present at the meeting will be

Peter West, personnel director, who is 53 years old. He has a law degree and was company secretary before transferring to his present position a year ago.

Tom Street, personnel manager, is 37 and joined Bryanston nine months ago from another firm where he was staff personnel manager.

David Bloomfield, personnel officer (head office) is also aged 37. He joined the company from school without the benefit of a good education and came up 'the hard way'.

William Green, personnel officer (factory) is 56 years old and was promoted to his present position after spending 20 years working on the factory floor.

Stuart Blake, training and safety officer, is a graduate engineer with a post-graduate diploma in education. He came to the company straight from university and is now 25 years old.

Selection interview — case study

One of the key functions of the personnel department is that of recruiting new employees and filling vacancies. It is by carefully planned recruitment and selection that a company ensures that it has the right people for the right jobs at the right time. It is not always easy to assess someone's suitability for a job, and the interviewer must use all the information he has available to make a balanced judgement. He probably refers a short list of candidates to the relevant departmental manager to make the final choice.

Take this case where the position of salesman or saleswoman at the XYZ Company Limited of Dagford has been advertised both within the company and in the local paper. The *personnel officer* in charge of recruitment for the marketing department has sifted through the applications and chosen 12 who seem suitable for interview. This he has done on the basis of qualifications, and experience or likely potential. The interviews have been arranged and the first applicant, *Charles Haughton*, is coming to meet him this afternoon.

Application Form XYZ Company Ltd

Position: Salesman
Surname: Haughton
Forenames: Charles Jeremy
Nationality: British
Year and date of birth: 6.3.52
Marital status: Single
Dependents: None
Medical history: None

Education

School	Years attended (dates)	Examination results (with grades)
Glyn Grammar School.	1963 - 1970	'O' levels, Maths, English Lang, History, Geography, French, Biology 'A' levels, English (B) History (C)

Further Education

University or college	Years attended	Examination results or qualifications
University of Hull	1970 - 1973	General Arts Degree

Employment

Employer	From	To	Position & duties	Reason for leaving
Smith & Brown	1973 - 1976		Graduate Trainee Salesman (soft drinks)	Wanted to move from fast moving consumer goods.
IBK Typewriters Ltd	1976 - 1980		Salesman (typewriters)	Tired of typewriters

Leisure interest .... Squash, Tennis, Member of Local Golf Club.

References .... Sales Manager, Mr. Goodnight, IBK Typewriters Ltd, Dagford.

Signature *C. J. Haughton*   Date 12. 2. 80.

Before the interview he studies all the available information on Mr Haughton, taken from his job application form and curriculum vitae if there is one. He also looks at the description of the position to be filled and plans the interview.

During the interview he takes care to put the applicant at his ease and gives him precise details of the job. He encourages him to talk about his previous jobs, his schooling and interests and observes his manner and approach. Finally he tells him when he will hear if he is required for a further interview.

(The job application form submitted by Charles Haughton is shown on page 43.)

Act out the interview in pairs or with one pair acting and others observing. The interview should last at least 15 minutes. Then make a critical assessment of each other's roles as interviewer and interviewee.

Discuss these assessments and draw up, as a group, a list of the 10 most important points each should bear in mind when giving or attending an interview.

Background information

The XYZ Company Limited of Dagford, a semi-industrial suburb on the outskirts of London, employs about 1500 people in light engineering: (staff 500, works 1000). It is an old-established, reputable company which for years was the foremost employer in the district. Recently other local industries have developed and even though XYZ maintains its good reputation, other firms offering similar rates of pay and employee benefits are providing keen competition for staff of all types. Employees come from a wide area — some live locally or in nearby villages, but some travel quite long distances from London and other suburbs.

Management Services

6

Outline of the function

The management services department is concerned with company efficiency — efficiency of information flow and processing, of organisation of work and of decision-making. As companies grow and their operations increase in complexity, so does the importance of management services.

Management services range from a single work study officer in a small factory to a major department headed by a senior manager and containing thousands of pounds worth of computer equipment, as is found in many large firms today. Basically it covers four main areas.

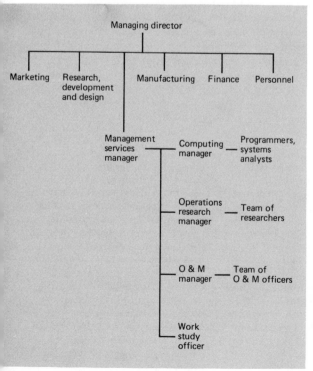

Computers and data processing

This section uses computers to process the mass of data a modern business — whether it be a manufacturing, retailing or commercial organisation — produces and uses. It includes systems analysts and computer programmers, responsible respectively for designing computer systems and writing these into computer language. The company may have its own computer or employ the services of one of the large bureaus such as IBM or ICL with a direct link to one of their computer centres.

The computing department may be involved in controlling manufacturing processes; stocks and sales; assisting with financial analysis; and paying wages. This type of work is expanding more rapidly than any other in modern industry, and, as computer applications become more widespread and the machines themselves become cheaper, it is likely to continue to do so.

Operational research

Staff in this area develop models and simulations to aid decision-making in production planning, marketing evaluation, machine maintenance and stock control. The operational researcher might work out a model to help answer the question: 'How much raw material should we buy, and how often, to keep up with the variable demands of the production process without tying up too much money in stocks and creating storage problems?' The information provided by the model would then be used by management as a basis for its decisions on stock purchases.

Organisation and methods (O & M)

This section is concerned with the implementation of more effective systems and their routine operation once installed. The emphasis is on the clerical side of the business — order forms, sales slips and invoices, for example. The O & M team would examine the flow of such documents and suggest ways of streamlining it and reducing unnecessary paper work. They may be involved in plant and office layout, payment and filing systems and production planning.

An example of O & M at work in the commercial world would be an investigation into the flow of customers through a bank. When you arrive at your local bank to draw out some money, you will probably take your place in the shortest queue. By what is apparently a trick of fate you may then watch the long queues on either side of you rapidly diminish while the customer at the head of your queue pays in vast sums of cash in small change, or, perhaps, has a lengthy chat with the cashier about the weather. It was the O & M people who in some larger banks suggested customers should all queue in one place,

taking their turns as the desks became vacant. Alternatively in some branches a special place for quick withdrawals was suggested as a feasible solution. The latest development is to dispense with cashier service altogether for straightforward transactions and have cash machines instead — often outside the door.

Work study

This is the most traditional branch of management services with its somewhat unjust image of people with stop watches spying from around corners. It is true that work study is concerned with improving productivity and reducing cost, but this is done as far as possible by eliminating unnecessary effort and installing more efficient working methods.

Work study uses two techniques

- Method study, which consists of observing existing working methods and trying to devise more efficient alternatives
- Work measurement, which breaks down jobs into their component parts and assesses how long these take, sometimes for use as a basis of determining payment.

Even more than the other service departments in a company, management services relies on goodwill and co-operation to put its ideas into practice. Computerisation may be seen as a threat to jobs. Changes to working methods often result in resentment amongst those who have 'always done it this way'. It is an area where not only a high degree of technical skill but also considerable diplomacy is required.

Profiles

John Yelland, project controller, data processing planning and co-ordination, Lloyds Bank

John Yelland's official title at Lloyds Bank is as long as his job is big. He is responsible for looking at the bank's computer needs for up to eight years in the future and seeing how these can best be met. This is an enormous task when one remembers that the London clearing banks are among the largest users of computers in the U.K. and without these machines our banking system would become entangled in paperwork.

John has seen tremendous advances in the use of computers in banking since he started work in a branch of Lloyds in 1955. It was not until 11 years later when he transferred to Lloyd's head

office in the City as a member of the organisation department that he became fully involved in this side of the bank's business. Since then his career has developed away from general banking, and he is now an expert in the world of computers.

At the end of the 1960s John was involved with the computerisation of the Bank's clearing system. 'This was an interesting development as it was the first time that a major change had been introduced into an area which was already fully computerised,' says John.

This experience provided a valuable background for his next appointment

as senior section manager, cheque clearings, where his task was to reduce the number of cheques rejected by automatic sorting equipment. In 1974 he was transferred to data processing operations department where he took charge of a computer room running the IBM computers that support half the bank's computer network. He was later given responsibility for planning and installing a new computer centre which was designed around two identical computers — each taking half the load.

Lloyds has been somewhat of a pioneer in the computerisation of British banking.

'In 1970 we became the first clearing bank to link all of its branches to a computer. Then seven years ago we launched another technological breakthrough with the installation of 'Cashpoint' – a computer linked cash dispenser – and we now have the largest on line cash dispenser network in the western world.'

John's role in all of this is to look at computers on the drawing board and compare their capabilities with the Bank's forecasted future needs.

'In essence mine is an advance planning operation. It is essential to ensure that all the many facets of banking are taken into account. Growth patterns have to be monitored to make sure that targets are being met. Plans need to be flexible enough to be changed as circumstances vary. We are constantly measuring up-to-date statistics against the projected plan.'

Computer advances are so rapid nowadays that the machinery is quickly outdated. John must keep in close contact with the manufacturers of computers and microprocessors in order to keep abreast of the latest available developments. Forward planning projects often involve a working party from Lloyds together with a manufacturer looking at existing methods of dealing with banking business, identifying future needs and coming up with a plan and a timetable to meet those needs.

In his quest to keep the Bank up-to-date with the latest machinery to meet its ever-growing needs John examines equipment worth millions of pounds. As he makes his decisions, he must always bear in mind that the growth of the company is very much related to economic conditions, so careful cost control and budgeting of expenditure must come into every plan.

All in all John Yelland is trying to make accurate predictions in a highly

unpredictable and expensive market. After all the major developments of recent years automation of the banking industry is not slowing down but proceeding faster than ever as customers

demand an ever more efficient service. One of the few areas where developments are moving with even greater speed is in the computer industry – and his work lies between the two.

Linda Gaskin, computer programmer, Metal Box

Linda Gaskin is a programmer in the computer services department of the Metal Box management systems division at Worcester. The programmer produces computer 'software' by writing coded

instructions which tell the machines – the 'hardware' – how to perform.

Linda joined the company in October 1976 as a graduate trainee.

'I spent the first week reading manuals and looking at existing programs, but was soon given by first program to write. I had a lot of help from other programmers and was closely supervised until I became used to the techniques involved. This was very useful. I certainly didn't find that it limited my scope. It enabled me to move gradually towards a position where I could work on my own. I didn't want to be dropped in at the deep end. This hasn't happened.'

Linda works on applications programs, which are sets of instructions designed to make the computer achieve a particular purpose, for example to prepare a payroll — still probably the most widespread use of computers in industry — or analyse sales. The other group of programmers are systems programmers who determine the way the computer organises itself — its workload, printing and storage.

'Applications programs at Metal Box are mostly written in Cobol and I have been on a course in Cobol programming, but of course it is only practice which makes one fluent in the language.

'The first major programs I worked on were all concerned with a project at Speke factory, which is part of the Paper and Plastics group, printing labels for cans, among other things. The project concerned a system of keeping stock records developed by the management systems department.

'The factories enter data at their sites on visual display units. These terminals are all linked to the computer at Worcester. The data is processed and used to update the existing records. The factories can then look at the records on the screens for the information they need. The records are kept up to date throughout the day.

'I have been involved with most of the programs required for the implementation of the Speke project. A lot of testing is needed before they can be put

into production. You have to be patient and to be prepared to trace through the steps of the program yourself if difficulties arise. Of course it helps to be aware of all possible problems at the start so that the chance of things going wrong after the program has gone into production is reduced.

'When development and testing is completed it is satisfying to see and know the program is working, especially when you have been able to become deeply involved with the project from start to finish.'

Programmers usually work in small teams, and it is not necessary for them to have a great deal of contact with the other sections of the company that will eventually use their programs. This is left to the systems analyst who, through close liaison with the user, will brief the programmer on what is required. Linda, however, likes to have a chance to visit the factories that use their systems. 'It makes the work more meaningful,' she says.

As for Linda's future . . . . As new graduates are recruited, Linda will move towards becoming a more senior programmer, and there is always scope for transferring into other fields such as systems analysis.

What computers do

Computers have become part of everyday life; the computer-printed payslip, bank statement or electricity bill is a familiar sight. Today, the sheer number of people cashing cheques, reserving travel tickets, etc. makes it practically impossible for routine work to be handled without high-powered machine help. Britain's four largest clearing banks, for example, handle and clear

about a million cheques every working day. Without the massive help a computer gives in processing these this would be a hopelessly slow and expensive task. This is also true for countless administrative and scientific tasks in many other businesses.

Here are four examples of the way computers are used in British industry.

Central Electricity Generating Board
Mike Sprackling, senior engineer

'In 1978/9 the Central Electricity Generating Board will spend in excess of £2000m on the consumption of coal, oil and gas fuels in meeting all demands for electricity instantaneously every minute of the day.

'In order to keep the total cost of electricity production to a minimum the operation of the CEGB's vast network of transmission lines and power stations must be closely planned to ensure maxi-

mum efficiency. This requires extensive computer assistance.

'On-line data processing computers at the national and local grid control centres gather information on the state of switch-gear and transmission equipment throughout England and Wales, and power flows on the transmission network are continuously monitored. Faults and breakdowns are relayed instantly to the control rooms.

'Off-line computing systems with visual display units in control rooms and planning offices throughout the

country enable engineers to communicate with the main Computing Centre and give access to large banks of stored data and suites of very powerful computed programs. These enable planning engineers to predict operating conditions on the grid system. Studies are undertaken to ensure that the power system, which throughout the year will have plant and equipment out of commission for maintenance, construction or breakdown, can be operated to meet the high standards of security.'

British Airways
Dorothy Boardman, assistant supervisor

'When you meet me at Victoria Air Terminal, you'll probably already have a computer-printed ticket produced by British Airways' reservations system, a part of one of the largest and most advanced commercial computing systems in the world. And although 70 per cent of the computer's capacity is taken up with pensions, payrolls, stock control, accounting and so on, it's still big enough to help us book and fly 14 million passengers around the world every year. The reservations system alone can book you onto a plane practically anywhere in just a few seconds — sometimes split seconds — because the system is designed to handle about 60 'messages' every second, and flash the reply to a visual display screen. For me, the system saves all the leafing through different manuals to answer each passenger enquiry, and keeping manuals up-to-date is time consuming. This screen replies to my instructions almost immediately, and gives me much more help than I've ever had before.'

Mothercare Limited
Harold C. Sanderson, director of computer systems

'Few people realise how difficult it is for shops to work out exactly what they've sold without repeatedly counting the stocks on the shelves and checking through records. It's a tedious job, and not very accurate because people get bored while they're doing it. So

Mothercare shops don't work that way. We have 180 shops in Britain, plus 22 on the continent, and since 1964 we've been using our computer to help us calculate, buy and distribute the stocks we need, and that's an order worth £1½m every week. We try to use the computer in as many other areas as we can — it helps ease the clerical workload in the mail order department for example, and no typist here would type address labels over and over again — a simple computer program to do that takes just a few seconds to run, so why waste our time? We were one of the first retail groups to use computer systems as a basis for our operations, yet it works in a very straight-forward manner. Each Mothercare item is given a 'line number' to represent its size, colour and type. We punch these line numbers onto tags which are sent to the suppliers of our merchandise — about 99 per cent of which is 'own brand'. Our manufacturers attach the tags to the goods, and dispatch them direct to our shops. Then as the merchandise is sold or put on the shelves, staff detach the tags and post them back to head office. Here they're fed in a batch into the computer, which can read the line number on each tag, and so calculate what needs re-ordering. The computer is programmed to re-order merchandise automatically by printing out the week's orders to suppliers, cheques to pay for them, and delivery instructions. The next day, each store receives a computer-printed list of what's on order so that staff can cross off items as they arrive. And that's really all the paperwork that's necessary — no invoices, no statements and no bought ledger to check.'

Rolls-Royce Limited
Tony Hodgson, divisional spares H.Q. manager

'Rolls-Royce are pledged to supply all aero-engine parts, within a certain time, for virtually all the gas turbines they have ever made — whether it's a new RB211 jet, or a turbo-prop Dart. We carry stocks of parts at our maintenance bases but some of their repairs involve 20-year-old engines — so you can see the scale of our parts supply requirements, and the need for tight control. We can't afford to carry vast stocks of rarely used, expensive parts, but neither can our customers afford a grounded plane — a £25m Tristar might need seven or more flying hours per day to earn its keep. The annual value of spares sales from the Derby plant alone is around £175m and we stock 80 000 individual components — for safety reasons we keep track of each major part, each engine and each plane. The mass of detailed information is stored by our computer system, which also uses information on spares sales to help forecast parts usage — a vital task when so much cash is at stake, but no easy matter as 85 per cent of the items we stock have no regular demand — and 60 per cent have no recent demand at all! So the computer's programming enables the system to consider many different factors before calculating the future demand for any single component. The computer helps us keep the tight control that's fundamental to our business. We're not the sort of company that can say 'Sorry, we don't make that any more!'

Source: After an IBM publication 'What computers do'.

Class activity

Post room reorganisation — case study*

Quite simple changes in the manner and order in which jobs are done or the arrangement of a room can often increase the efficiency of a department. This can lead to considerable savings in costs. In a large company this 'method study' would be carried out by the management

*This exercise was prepared in collaboration with S. Cordell of the Cranfield School of Management.

services department; in a smaller concern outside consultants would probably be called in to deal with a specific problem.

Consider a wholesale and retail store dealing with small tools for engineers — for example micrometers and verniers. The management is concerned about the standard of the service provided by its post room — an

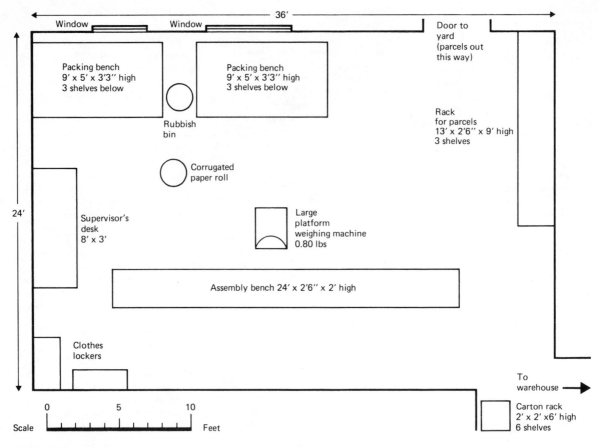

POST ROOM, existing layout

important part of the organisation because it is responsible for dispatching goods to customers. If parcels arrive late, goods damaged through poor packing, or items not ordered are dispatched, the image of the entire company suffers.

A team of organisation and methods consultants have been asked to look at the operation of the post room. Their findings follow.

Existing method

Items for each parcel are brought from the warehouse, checked against an assembly note, packed and weighed. The weight is recorded on the parcel and advice note, and the parcel put out for dispatch by GPO parcel post. A more detailed description of their method follows.

The sales office sends assembly notes containing lists of the items required for each parcel to the post room supervisor. A service operator collects six assembly notes at a time, gets the items required and takes them by trolley to the post room, where he leaves them with the notes on the assembly bench. Each trip takes an

average of nine minutes. The layout of the post room is shown in the figure above.

A packer goes to the assembly bench and checks the goods against the assembly note to see that the items brought by the operator are correct. He takes the assembly note to the supervisor's desk and collects an advice note and labels for the parcel. He goes back to the assembly bench, picks up the goods for the parcel and carries them to his packing bench. After that he walks over to the roll of corrugated paper and cuts off the length required to wrap the parcel. He then goes to the carton rack, selects the appropriate size carton, goes back to his bench and makes up the carton. Then he wraps the carton in brown paper, fixes a label on the parcel and ties it up with string. The paper and string are kept on the packers' bench. He then takes the parcel to the weighing machine, weighs it and returns with it to his bench. He records the weight on the advice note and the parcel. Finally, he takes the parcel to the rack for dispatch and the advice note to the supervisor's desk. Then he goes to the assembly bench to repeat the process.

Further information

Arrival of assembly notes	11 per cent at 0700, 81 per cent at 1000 and 8 per cent at 1400
Time taken to pack parcel	Average 5½ minutes
Average number of parcels	180 per day
Types of goods packed	Micrometers, verniers, taps and dies, dial gauges
Parcel collections by GPO	1630 daily
Staffing	1 supervisor (part-time with other duties) 3 packers (2 full-time, 1 from 1400 only) 1 service operator (full-time)
Hours of work	Monday–Thursday: 0700–1700 Friday: 0700–1600 Breaks: 0930–0945, 1200–1310 and 1500–1515 Overtime starts at 1600
Payment	Basic rate £1.25 per hour (excluding supervisor) Overtime at time and a half.

A flow chart showing the existing operations is given in the next column and a statement of annual costs is given in the table below. Note that the supervisor and service operator are not included under labour costs since the exercise is concerned with the work of the post-room only.

Statement of Annual Costs, existing method

	£	£
Labour		
2 men @ £2990 p.a.	5 980	
1 man @ £1040 p.a.	1 040	
	7 020	7 020
Materials		
Brown paper	300	
Corrugated paper	3 000	
String	400	
	3 700	3 700
Total cost, labour and materials		10 720

Annual costs are based on a five-day week, 48 working-week year (43 000 parcels).

FLOW CHART OF PACKER PACKING PARCEL — EXISTING METHOD

Chart begins: Goods and assembly notes on assembly bench. Packer at assembly bench.
Chart ends: Parcel packed in store. Packer at assembly bench.

Key ◯ = Operation ▢ = Inspection
⇒ = Transport ④ = Operation number 4

Distance moved

	(1)	Select assembly note.
	[1]	Check goods with assembly note.
16'	⇒1	Take assembly note to desk.
	(2)	Collect delivery advice note.
16'	⇒2	Return to assembly bench.
	(3)	Collect goods for parcel.
10'	⇒3	Take goods to packing bench.
	(4)	Deposit goods on packing bench.
6'	⇒4	To roll of corrugated paper.
	(5)	Cut off length.
6'	⇒5	Return to bench.
	(6)	Deposit corrugated paper.
28'	⇒6	To carton rack.
	(7)	Select carton.
28'	⇒7	Return to bench.
	(8)	Make up carton.
	(9)	Wrap goods in corrugated paper.
	(10)	Pack in carton.
	(11)	Wrap in brown paper.
	(12)	Stick on label.
	(13)	Tie parcel with string.
6'	⇒8	Take parcel to weighing machine.
	[2]	Weigh parcel.
6'	⇒9	Return to bench.
	(14)	Record weight on advice note and parcel.
16'	⇒10	Take parcel to rack.
	(15)	Take advice note to desk.
31'	⇒11	Place parcel in rack.
	(16)	Place advice note on desk.
16'	⇒12	Go to assembly bench for further parcel.

Summary

◯	Operations	16
▢	Inspections	2
⇒	Transports	12
	Total number of steps in process	30
	Distance travelled	185'

O & M team brief

(1) You are O & M consultants. How would you improve the method and layout of the post room within the following constraints set by management?

- No structural alterations to the room are permissible.
- Modifications, additions or disposal of equipment is permissible, provided a balance is maintained between cost and savings.
- The supervisor may not be used for packing or service work.
- No expansion of work is envisaged.

(2) Prepare a new flow chart and post room layout for your proposed method.
(3) Draw up a projected statement of annual costs and a statement of the non-recurring charges of the investigation. Your own charge for the investigation is £300.
(4) Make a 10-minute presentation to the management team justifying your recommendations.

Introducing a mini-computer — case study

The employees of a company are often wary of the introduction of techniques and equipment aimed at improving efficiency. Consider this case of a small clothing manufacturer.

Background information

On the advice of a firm of management consultants and their own management services officer, the board of directors of Babywear Limited has decided that it would be sound business practice to install a mini-processor, which would automatically issue invoices to customers. At present this is done manually and tends to be both slow and costly, particularly because much of the firm's business is from a large number of small orders.

The managing director sends out the following memo, drafted by the management services officer, to all departmental managers.

'The company has decided to install a mini-processor to issue invoices to customers. This will arrive next month. It is important that all departments are prepared for the change so that work is disrupted as little as possible.'

This succinct message meets with a variety of responses.

The *manufacturing manager* assumes this will not affect his department so he leaves it in his in-tray and ignores it.

The *financial manager*, who was involved in the initial discussions with the consultants, is all in favour of using new technology. He invites a representative of the computer supplier, which is selling them the mini-processor, to speak to his staff about what the machine can do and how it will affect their work. The sales rep is also able to answer any questions they may have.

The *marketing manager* is responsible for salesmen who are travelling all over the country. He doesn't think this change justifies bringing them all in for a chat. He does, however, explain to those to whom he speaks on the telephone what is going on because the firm's customers will notice something is different when they receive printed invoices. But he doesn't think it will affect the customers much.

The *administrative manager* is highly suspicious of the whole idea. His department has been sending out invoices and dispatching goods for years and he cannot recall when he last had a complaint from a customer about the service. Also, he suspects that this might lead to some of his department being made redundant, but he does not check on this in case he has to be the one to tell them.

(In fact the management services officer and personnel manager have worked out that no one will lose his job. The board has decided to expand their sales area during the following year and to try to capture several extra orders from further afield. The introduction of the mini-processor is part of an overall plan to streamline their operation and increase the amount of work the service section can cope with. Staff currently handling invoices will be fully occupied dealing with the increased number of queries, which the greater number of orders the company hopes to receive will inevitably generate. If anything, this anticipated increase in production, due to the more efficient service to customers the firm can provide, may lead to their having to take on more staff. Management decides, however, not to tell the employees of this as it might lead to rumours).

The administrative manager, therefore, simply calls in his office supervisor, who is in charge of the invoice clerks, and, like him, has been with the firm since it started. She immediately assumes that her girls' jobs are threatened and her boss does not categorically deny this. She decides to put as many spanners in the works as she can to ensure that 'the computer' does not work satisfactorily, and management will therefore see how indispensable she and her staff are.

Within a few days everyone on the site has heard of the impending arrival of 'that machine', and ideas on what it is intended to do and why it has been bought are colourful and varied. In fact one shop steward first hears of the change from his union members in the manufacturing department who inform him that management has decided to bring in a computer to control the production lines and at least half of them are likely to lose their jobs. He calls a meeting of all shop stewards to agree on what action they should take.

One way and another everyone has decided whether the new arrival is going to be a help or a hindrance, but few, except the finance department, are prepared for the changes it will in fact make to their work and its organisation.

Discussion

Consider the following questions.

(1) Do you think the use of the mini-processor will help the firm in the short term? in the long term?

(2) Will it be well received in the factory? If not, why not?

(3) What went wrong with the communication of the decision to install it? Prepare a plan of action for management to follow to communicate the decision effectively and get maximum co-operation from all departments.

Decision-making in Industry

7

Introduction

Chapters 1–6 have through brief descriptions and examples looked at the roles played by the various sections of a company in the production process. In this final chapter of Part 1 we look at two case studies in detail.

The first is about an entrepreneur who is thinking of setting up his own business; it describes the type of decisions he must take and the information he has available on which to base these decisions. The second is a business simulation which tries to bring into the classroom an idea of the decisions that managers face during the day-to-day operation of their businesses. In neither case is there a clear-cut solution. The decisions are surrounded by ifs, buts and maybes — just as they are when they are taken in the world outside.

Class activity

Charles Morning, publisher — case study*

Background information

Charles Morning has worked for several years as publishing manager with a large firm of book publishers. For the last two years he has been considering starting his own business publishing specialised technical textbooks. His wife, Catherine, who has a secretarial training, would like to help him.

In particular Charles feels that being able to take

* This case study was prepared by Joe Townsley, an accountant, a lecturer in finance at the University of Manchester Institute of Technology and a director of Polytech Publishers Limited, for the Careers Research and Advisory Council (CRAC) Insight Programme.

full responsibility for all decisions in his own firm would give him real satisfaction. He appreciates that, at least in the foreseeable future, in comparison with his present job he will have to work longer hours and there will be nobody to take over if he is ill.

There are good prospects in his present job with the likelihood of a seat on the board in about five years. He receives a salary of £7000 per annum with a non-contributory pension scheme (all contributions are paid by his employer at the rate of 10 per cent of his salary) and a new 1300cc car is provided every two years. He expects to be able to keep his current car if he pays £1200 for it when he leaves.

In assessing the resources which he has available to put into the business Charles has noted the following:

- He owns a four bedroom detached house which has a market value of £30 000 and on which he has a mortgage outstanding of £10 000.
- He has recently inherited securities which, if they were sold on the market at today's prices, would realise £10 000.
- Catherine also owns securities with a market value of £10 000.

Charles agrees to sell his securities and use the £10 000 as capital to start the business. His wife has £10 000 for when it is needed. They both agree that they will need at least £4800 per annum in cash from the business to live on.

Running the publishing business

Charles Morning must also consider how much money he needs to run the business. He would first have to obtain suitable premises. The cost of renting premises with a small warehouse and offices would be at least £10 000 per annum. This does not appear to be economically feasible to Charles at this stage. Alternatively they could rent a small warehouse near his house for about £2400 and use his home as an office. In the first year of operation he estimates that he and his wife could manage the packing and distribution of the books themselves; thereafter they would have to employ someone else. The general overheads, such as telephone, insurance, car and so forth, are likely to amount to £1500 in the first year.

For the type of books he intends to publish Charles Morning would follow the customary practice of publishers. His authors would write a manuscript for him in consideration of a royalty of 10 per cent of the selling price of the book. Booksellers would receive 30 per cent of the selling price as their margin. For example, if the price of a book were £1, receipts would break down as follows:

	£
Retailer's margin	0.30
Author's royalty	0.10
Publisher's share	0.60
	1.00

The bookseller is invoiced at the selling price less 30 per cent and will normally pay for goods two months after dispatch. The author's royalty is calculated on an annual basis and paid four months after the end of the accounting period. For example, if the value of sales of a book in the year ended 31 December were £1000, the author would receive his royalties (of £100) on the following 1 May.

The costs of packing and forwarding books are now substantial and, based on his experience with his current employer, Charles estimates that this cost would amount to an average of £0.50 per book sold, payable immediately upon sale.

Once he has agreed to publish an author's manuscript, the publisher must select a printer to produce the book at a reasonable cost and to the specification of the publisher. The publisher pays the printer and takes the finished books into his stores until they are distributed.

To be profitable a publisher must be able to identify a marketable manuscript. He will advise the author about the content and length of the book as well as its format, type and binding. The publisher will edit the finished manuscript, make decisions on layout and give technical instructions to the printer. Finally he must decide how many are to be printed.

Usually books are unique products. In the technical area that Charles Morning hopes to enter there is often a fairly specific market — for example, Chemistry 'A' level students — and there will be competing books aimed at the same market. Whether a book will become a best seller is difficult to predict. Most authors of best sellers had several rejections by publishers before their first book was accepted. However, a good publisher can judge whether there is a market for a technical book.

In printing a new book there are 'fixed' costs which are not related to the quantity of books produced. Setting the manuscript into type is likely to be the largest of these, but there is also the cost of preparing the machinery prior to a production run. Fixed costs will remain the same whether one copy or a million copies are produced. In addition there will be 'variable' costs which are related to the actual number of books produced. The cost of paper and other materials used will be one such cost; another will be the cost of labour time expended on the printing and binding machines. This variable cost is usually lower per book for large print runs.

Cash Flow Projection

	Jan	Feb	Mar	April	May	June	July	Aug	Sept	Oct	Nov	Dec	Total
(1) Sales (number of books)	–	–	–	–	–	–	100	100	100	100	100	100	600
(2) Retail selling price per book							5	5	5	5	5	5	
Cash received (£)													
(3) Cash from sales, i.e. (2) less 30%, delayed by 2 months									350	350	350	350	1 400
(4) Capital from Charles Morning	10 000												10 000
(5) Catherine Morning	–	–	–	–	–	–	–	–	–	–	–	–	–
(6) Total cash receipts	10 000												
Cash payments (£)													
(7) Postage and packing							50	50	50	50	50	50	300
(8) Rent		200	200	200	200	200	200	200	200	200	200	200	2 400
(9) General overheads		125	125	125	125	125	125	125	125	125	125	125	1 500
(10) Purchase of car	1 200												1 200
(11) Cash withdrawn	400	400	400	400	400	400	400	400	400	400	400	400	4 800
(12) Payment for books	–	–	–	–	–	–	–	–	–	–	–	–	
(13) Total cash payments	1 925	725	725										
(14) Net change i.e. (6) – (13)	+8 075	–725	–725										
(15) Balance from previous month	0	8 075	7 350										
(16) Balance	8 075	7 350	6 625										

You are required to complete lines (12) and (5) and then fill in the totals for (6), (13), (14), (15) and (16). The first three months are already completed to guide you.

Charles Morning has just received some quotations from printers on a manuscript prepared by an old friend who is an established author. The lowest quote for this book is as follows.

Chemistry for 'A' level students

Estimate length (pages)	650

Costs	£
Film typsetting @ £5 per page	3250
Materials per 1000	550
Printing text and covers for the first 1000	850
for every additional 1000	175
Binding in limp covers for the first 1000	700
for every additional 1000	400

Printers require payment within one month of delivery.

Printing Costs (£)

Quantity	1 000	2 000	5 000
Typesetting	3 250		
Materials	550		
Printing	850		
Binding	700		
Total cost	5 350		
Cost per book	5.35		

Charles has had some preliminary discussions with David Green, a chartered accountant with whom he occasionally plays golf. David has suggested that initially a careful estimate of cash requirements should be made on a month-by-month basis, as well as an estimate of the profit or loss to be made in the first year. Longer-term prospects should then be considered. In order to complete these estimates Charles Morning has made the following assessment of likely future activity.

- In his first year he estimates that he can obtain copies of the chemistry book on 30 June (that is, he allows six months for production of the finished book).
- Because there is a competing chemistry book on the market the maximum retail selling price which could be charged with any hope of success would be £5 a copy.
- Assuming that the selling price were to be fixed at £5, he estimates that sales invoiced between 1 July and 31 December would be 600 books and in each of the following two years the total would be 2000 books. Thereafter sales would die away or increase substantially depending on whether the customers really liked the product.
- For each new book he estimates that 200 inspection copies will be given free of charge to prospective customers.
- In each year after the first he expects to publish four new books similar to the chemistry book in production costs, number of pages, number of illustrations, etc.

Statement of Profit and Loss for the year ended 31 December

£	£		£	£
3 000		Sales 600 books @ £5		3 000
	900	Less: Retailers' discounts	900	
1 200	300	Royalties to authors	300	1 200
1 800		Net sales value		1 800
		Less: Cost of books sold		
	5 350	Books purchased (. . . . books @ £ . . . . a copy)	. . .	
	1 070	Less: stock of books at December 31[1]	. . .	
	4 280		. . .	
3 210	1 070	Less: Inspection Copies given away (200 copies)	. . .	. . . .
(1 410)		Gross profit (loss)		. . . .
		Less Expenses		
	1 070	Cost of inspection copies (as above)	. . .	
	300	Distribution and packing	. . .	
	2 400	Rent	. . .	
	1 500	General overheads	. . .	
	200	Depreciation of car[2]	. . .	
10 270	4 800	Remuneration of Mr & Mrs Morning[3]	. . .	. . . .
£(11 680)		Net Profit (Loss)		. . . .

(1) This number is the amount the publisher has ordered less sales and inspection copies, i.e. less 800 copies.
(2) The car costing £1200 is expected to be used for two years when it will be sold for £800, i.e. (£1200 − £800) ÷ 2 = £200 depreciation per annum.
(3) This does not represent 'proper' remuneration. If the business is organised as a partnership the profit is calculated without allowance for the partners' salaries. The partners then draw from this profit.

Background Information for Business Simulation

1, *Balance Sheet*

When you take over the company is in the following financial position:

Liabilities	£	Assets	£
50 000 shares @ £1.00	50 000	Land and buildings	35 000
Profit and loss account	10 000	Plant and machinery	15 000
		Stocks (at cost)	8 000
		Cash in hand	2 000
	60.000		60 000

2. *Marketing*

Expenditure on marketing must be in multiples of £100 and will be used purely for advertising and sales promotion.

3. *Price*

The selling price can only be set in multiples of £1.00.

4. *Costs*

Production costs are made up of two parts

- Indirect costs (overheads), which are £3000 at present, and
- Direct costs which vary according to the amount produced as follows

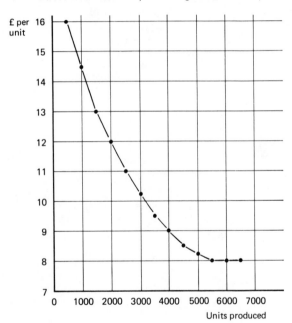

Graph to show the variation of direct cost with number of units made.

5. *Production*

Units produced are placed in stock and available for sale at the end of each quarter. Maximum production (limited by machine) capacity) is 3000 units per quarter, representing normal output for a five-day week for three months.

6. *Stock*

Operation of stock is on a first in, first out basis (FIFO). The value of stock for manufacturing purposes is the total manufacturing cost per unit. You have 3000 units in stock at the beginning of the year.

7. *Bought out items*

If you have insufficient stock to meet the sales for any quarter, these must be bought out at the average price quoted by competitors.

The tables on cash flow and annual profit and loss are of the form suggested by David Green. However Charles has still not decided how many copies of the books should be printed in the first instance.

The exercise

Consider the following points:

(1) What form of business organisation should be adopted? Should Charles Morning start off as a sole trader, in partnership or as a limited company?
(2) Complete a schedule such as that of the table on page 57.
(3) Decide on the number of books Charles Morning should order.
(4) Complete the two tables on pages 56 and 57 on the basis of how many books you think should be ordered.
(5) Is the finance available likely to be sufficient? Where could extra finance be found?
(6) Will the business be profitable in future years?
(7) Is the venture likely to be worthwhile?

A business simulation

The aim of the exercise is to set objectives for your company and try to meet these by making decisions on the way it is to operate during the year. These reflect the decisions which have to be made by boards of directors in industry.

Divide the class into five groups, each of which acts as the newly-appointed board of directors of a manufacturing company. These five companies are in competition. Each board has a free hand in making decisions on the running of the company.

On the basis of the decisions made each quarter by the five competing companies, their results for the quarter are assessed. You can then see how far you have been able to meet your original objectives, and whether these initial objectives were the best for the long-term prospects of the company.

Background information

First read through the details about your company and its operation which are given in the table on page 58. Make sure you are quite clear what this information means.

Setting objectives

Each group then has five to ten minutes to decide upon the company's two main objectives for the coming year.

Some examples may be

- To make the highest possible profit
- To capture a certain percentage of the market
- To maintain full employment

or any others you feel are important. Write these down and hand them in.

Decisions for the first quarter

Next you have 20 minutes to set the following for the operation of the company for the first quarter:

- Production target
- Marketing expenditure
- Selling price.

The total sales of all five companies for the previous year are given in the table below.

Total Sales Volume for Previous Year

First quarter	14 000
Second quarter	12 000
Third quarter	10 000
Fourth quarter	6 500

The selling price is governed by your manufacturing costs (direct and indirect), the amount spent on marketing and your agreed profit margin. Remember that the companies have the existing stocks to sell as well as what you decide to produce for the quarter. When you have reached agreement on the three factors, record them on a decision sheet such as that in the figure below and hand them in.

Example of a Decision Sheet

Company _____ Year _____

Decisions	Abbrev-iation	First quarter	Second quarter	Third quarter	Fourth quarter
Marketing (£s)	(A)				
Price (£ per unit)	(B)				
Production target (units)	(C)				

Results for the first quarter

The teacher now compares the decision sheets for the five companies and announces the results for the first quarter. Each company is told the total sales for the industry and its own share.

Decisions for the second quarter

This time you have additional information on which to base your decisions — your results from the previous quarter. In the next session you have about 15 minutes to do two things:

Example of Results Sheet

Year . . . .   Quarter . . . .   Company . . . .

Results

(D)   Industry sales   . . . .   units

(E)   Your share   . . . .   per cent

(F)   Company sales = (D) × (E) = ...   X . . . . = ... units

(G)   Direct cost per unit from graph on page 58   = £ . . . .

(H)   Total manufacturing cost per unit = (G) + $\dfrac{3000}{(C)}$ = ... + $\dfrac{3000}{....}$ = £ . . . . . .

Stock position: *units*

    Opening stock (J from previous quarter)

    Add production this quarter (C)   _____

    Total available for sale

    Less sales this quarter (F)   _____

    (J) Closing stock   _____

If J is negative . . . . items purchase @ £ . . . . each   (average competitor's price)

Costs   *Income*

Marketing (A)   £ . . . .

Manufacturing (H) × (C)   £ . . . .

Cost of purchased units   £ . . . .

                            _____   _____

      Total costs   £ _____   Sales (F) × (B)   = £ _____

      Result   _____

      Profit or loss

- Complete a results sheet such as that in the figure on page 60 for the first quarter to give an idea of your current position.
- Make the decisions on marketing, price and production targets for the second quarter.

Fill in the second column on the decision sheet for this quarter and hand it in.

Results for the second quarter

Again your share of the total market is announced and you can fill in a results sheet to see whether you have fared better or worse than in the first quarter, and assess whether you are meeting your original objectives.

Decisions and results for the third and fourth quarters

These are made in the same way so that at the end of the year you should have

- A decision sheet showing your decisions for each quarter
- Four results sheets, one for each quarter.

The year's results

You are now in a position to work out from your results sheets what your company has achieved and whether you have met your goals.

Answer the following questions for your company so that these can be recorded on a table for all five competing enterprises and you can see which has been the most successful.

(1) What was your total profit or loss for the year?
(2) What were your total sales?
(3) How did your production fluctuate during the year?
(4) How often were you out of stock?
(5) What dividend (pence per share) would you declare?

Assessing the companies

Looking at the results of the five companies, consider the following questions.

(1) Which do you think was the most successful company?
(2) Why is this one more successful?
(3) Who seems to have benefited most from the way each company has operated — the shareholders, the employees or the customers.
(4) Did your company meet its original objectives?
(5) If not, can you say why not?
(6) Do you still agree with the original objectives?

Annual general meeting

You might now hold an annual general meeting (AGM) for the most 'successful' company at which its board

- Announces its results for the year and comments on them
- Declares its annual dividend
- Explains its objectives for the past year and plans for the coming one.

Some other points to consider

(1) What return did your company give its shareholders on the money they invested in it?
(2) How does this compare with current building society interest rates?
(3) What value would you put on the shares of your company after a year's operation under its new board?
(4) Do you think people would invest in this company?
(5) Supposing you wanted to expand the company in the coming year, where would you find the money for the new machines and buildings, and to pay extra employees?
(6) How much tax do you think the company would have to pay on profits made during the year you have been looking at?

Part 2

Structure and Size

8

Structure

A company, whether large or small, is made up of a group of people with varied skills and talents who work together to achieve a goal. In a manufacturing company this is probably a production target; in a retailing one, a sales target; and in a service company, a level of efficiency of service to its customers.

The way the company employees are organised — how they are grouped under their various bosses — can make the difference between success and failure in reaching these targets.

What is likely to be the most satisfactory structure? Traditionally companies are based on a pyramid shape so that they have few 'chiefs' and plenty of 'indians'. A typical pyramid is shown opposite.

The company structure can be broken down into smaller pyramids until at the shop floor level it comprises small groups of employees, each team reporting to its individual leader. It is this leader, called the first-line supervisor, in whose hands the success of the

Board and managing director

Senior management team

Middle managers

First-line supervisors

Employees/shop floor

company in achieving its goals largely rests. It is he who has personal contact with the employees which, particularly in larger firms, senior management do not. He — by his own style of leadership — can get results by consulting his staff, setting them targets and dealing with their problems.

Class activity

School organisation — exercise

Draw up an organisation structure for your school, or use the details given in the two tables on page 66. These tables show the number of staff and pupils at various levels in a fictitious school which could be used as a basis for the exercise.

Staff

Position	Number
Teaching staff	
Headmistress	1
Deputy headmistress	1
Senior teacher/head of department	1
Heads of department	17
Full-time teaching assistants	13
Teachers in first year of training	4
Part-time teachers	13
Auxiliary staff	
Caretaker	1
Assistant caretaker	1
Cleaners	11
Groundsman	1
Kitchen staff	10
Dinner ladies	3

Pupils

Year	Forms	Number of pupils	Average group size
1	4	129	31
2	4	131	29
3	4	111	27
4	3	89	20
5	5	97	21
6/7/8	3	163	Variable

The group size for the three senior years depends on the subject demand in each year.

Governors

The school has a board of 13 governors.

Start with the headmaster or headmistress as the equivalent of the managing director and work right through the school, breaking each department into sub-groups in the way they would normally function. For the purpose of the analogy treat the students as the 'shop floor'. Consider the following questions:

(1) What are the numbers at each level in the pyramid?
(2) What is the ratio of 'managers' to 'workers'?
(3) What size are the groups a 'first-line supervisor' has to cope with? What are the limitations on this number?
(4) What is the task the school sets out to achieve? How adequate is the structure for achieving this task?
(5) Are there weaknesses in the structure — for example for communication or motivation. If so, what special arrangements are made to overcome these?

Company organisation — exercise

Now look at the organisation structure of Warpweft Limited, a medium-sized textile company in Southwest England employing 470 people. (The organisation structure is given below, figures in brackets show the numbers working in each department).

What factors decide company structure?

A few guidelines:

- The work group should not be too large for one person to manage.
- Nor should it be so small that the leader could do the jobs of all those reporting to him as well as his own.
- The fewer levels there are, the better.
- Deputies are best avoided as they confuse the line accountability.
- Groups should be organised according to their objective, so that all those involved in a specific project are grouped together.

An abbreviated organisation structure for Warpwept Limited

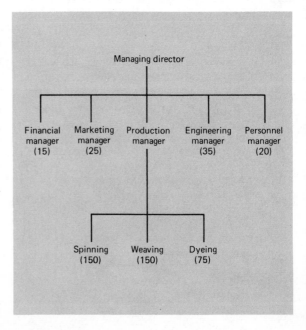

Some organisational complications

- Size
- Shifts
- Scattered factories
- Group companies with subsidiaries
- The need for floating pools of people
- The extent of automation and complexity of production processes.

It is worth noticing that if the head of the unit has 7 people reporting to him and each of them has 7, and that at the lowest level there are 12 to each leader, there is an organisation of 588 people with only 3 levels of leadership.

Consider the following:

(1) How many middle and junior managers would be needed to run Warpweft satisfactorily? How do you arrive at this figure?
(2) Will the size of groups reporting directly to one boss vary from one department or level to another? If so, what are the reasons for this?
(3) What is the main task of the company?
(4) Which would you consider to be the departments directly concerned with achieving the task and which are the service departments helping them in this objective?
(5) Compare this organisation with that for the school. Can you explain the differences?

Size

Companies seem to have a natural tendency to grow — by expansion, takeovers and sometimes mergers. There are many obvious advantages in increasing the size of an organisation, but also some disadvantages.

Advantages of large businesses

- Certain so called 'economies of scale' result from the pooling of resources
    Costs are spread more widely so that technical, managerial and selling costs are less per unit and consequently a lower price is often possible.
    There can be lower labour costs per unit produced.
- There is often more money available for
    Expensive and sophisticated machinery
    Extensive advertising
    Supporting research and development teams and piloting their experiments
    Social welfare facilities for employees and community projects

    Financing specialist personnel and training departments.
- Large businesses can make use of special terms and discounts.
- It is easier for them to raise capital and bank loans to finance further expansions, improvements to buildings and equipment and diversification.
- There is scope for mass production and division of labour.

Disadvantages of large businesses

- Large organisations can become unwieldy and inefficient with too many levels responsible for making decisions so that no one is clear who is accountable for what.
- They can be very impersonal to work in, making people feel like small rather unimportant cogs in a large wheel. This can lead to poor management—employee relations and communication may not be good.
- Customers may also find the organisation impersonal, which can affect sales.
- While having advantages in terms of cost and sometimes efficiency, mass production techniques such as assembly lines, can have their problems:
    They are less flexible when it comes to changes of product than smaller-scale assemblies

Production line jobs tend to be dull and monotonous, often resulting in serious difficulties with motivation, leading to frustration and low productivity.

Discussion

Consider the following:

(1) In what ways do large organisations overcome the problems of size? What examples can you find to illustrate your answers?
(2) Prepare a profile of the companies in your local area, stating their approximate sizes, the nature of their businesses and their products. Do any patterns emerge? If so, can you explain these?

Class activity

Tackling the size problem — case study

Brian Charlesworth, owner of a small firm in Essex making cardboard cartons, has decided the time has come to expand. He established the company six years ago and for the last four years orders have been flowing in thick and fast. His manufacturing process is simple. He buys in card ready printed and his staff of 25 cut and assemble the cartons and pack them ready for delivery to customers.

Brian deals with the selling himself; two clerks take orders by telephone. His wife acts as administration manager, dealing with the basic accounts and bookkeeping, stock control and personnel matters.

Brian secures a loan of £50 000 from an investment bank, topped up with a short-term loan from his bank manager. He then rents new premises and installs equipment that will allow him to do his own printing and increase his range of products. He recruits another 50 operators and takes on a full-time accountant, a printing manager, two extra clerks and two salesmen. He promotes his senior foreman to assembly manager and makes some of his longest-serving workers supervisors.

The problem

So far everything has gone according to plan, but within a month of operating his new plant the following problems occur.

- Two of his newly-promoted supervisors leave because they cannot cope with the additional responsibility.
- Problems arise with preparing the extra pay packets and a few times lately these have not been ready for pay-day.
- The new printing manager and the assembly manager fall out and the latter sends in his resignation.
- The levels of absenteeism and people taking sick leave seem far higher than ever before.
- Some of the orders for last month were not ready by delivery date and one long-standing customer is talking about taking his business elsewhere.
- When Brian goes into the works he finds the atmosphere strained. He sees many unfamiliar faces and no one seems to recognise him. He asks a few people how they are getting on, and no one can tell him what their production targets are or even to whom they should go if they have problems.
- He notices groups of people sitting around, apparently with nothing to do, and, on asking why, is told in a rather bored fashion that they have run out of card.
- His wife seems depressed and irritable and keeps muttering that they should have left the business as it was.

Discussion

(1) Has Brian Charlesworth created a monster out of a mouse?
(2) If you were in his shoes, what steps would you take to tackle the problems?

A closer look at one of the problems of size

One of the most serious difficulties of running large organisations is the fact that it is not possible for senior management to have personal contact with every employee. Ensuring good communication throughout the company in such circumstances is not easy.

Out of 35 stoppages which took place recently in a large organisation, 18 were due to failures of communication. The cost of these stoppages could not be measured in the hours lost alone; they upset the whole rhythm of production and lessened co-operation between employees and their managers.

Management has many methods available for filling the communication gap; for example

- Breaking down the whole into work groups, each with a leader who is responsible for communicating to his group
- Using company magazines
- Sending letters to employees
- Using loudspeakers or closed circuit television
- Arranging mass meetings
- Using notice boards.

All of these techniques have their uses and successful management is careful to make the most of them all, using the right method for the right type of message. The following case study illustrates this problem.

Class activity

The problem at Warpweft Limited — case study

The board of directors of Warpweft are concerned about a 10 per cent drop last year in sales; this was a result of price cuts by their biggest competitors.

They feel that if the company is to regain its former position and maintain it, they too must lower their prices. This can only be done if costs are also cut. They have evidence that some parts of the organisation are not as efficient as they ought to be, and they have decided to bring in a firm of consultants to conduct a survey into the efficiency of the whole company and to recommend further action.

The consultants have been engaged, and will be starting in one month's time. They will be making a complete tour of the works, asking questions of employees and supervisors at all levels.

There is a total of 480 employees, all on one site, and there is no shift working. There are three main production buildings, a separate office block housing senior executives and the personnel department and a small maintenance workshop.

The works are unionised, except for the staff side which has a joint consultative committee (see page 84).

All the usual mass media for communication are available. There is a staff dining room and a canteen. The organisation structure is shown below.

Discussion

It is now noon on Wednesday and the works shuts down for the three weeks' annual holiday at 1600 on Friday. The managing director considers that every person employed needs to understand the situation before the factory closes.

(1) What will be the consequences if everyone does not know why the consultants are coming?
(2) What methods of communication are available to management and what are the advantages and disadvantages of each?
(3) How would you, as the managing director of Warpweft, explain what is happening to the employees?

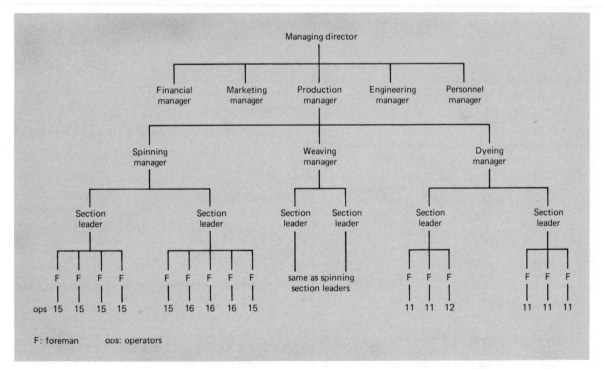

F: foreman   ops: operators

Management and Leadership

9

Wherever groups of people work together to achieve a task, the groups seem to function most efficiently when one member takes on the role of organising the others. Leaderless groups tend to lack purpose and direction.

Industry is no exception. In industry the people within the groups have specialised roles. In a steel works, for example, several hundred people are involved in the financing, manufacture, marketing and distribution of millions of tons of metal every year. The company employs accountants, operators, salesmen, fitters, typists, drivers and engineers, to name but a few. Someone must have an overall view of how all these different specialists work together, and this is the role of management.

The job of a manager, be he the managing director or a first-line supervisor, is to achieve results through the best use of resources available to him — of which not the least important is people. To do this effectively a manager must have

- technical competence
- administrative competence
- the ability to get the best out of people, or leadership ability.

His task is to get things done by organising the work of others. To do this he may do some or all of the following:

- Give instructions
- Communicate with and consult those who work under him
- Select new employees
- Train staff
- Check their work
- Set targets
- Appraise performance
- Discipline
- Dismiss
- Maintain morale.

His main activities can be grouped into five areas:

- Defining objectives
- Planning
- Co-ordinating
- Motivating and controlling
- Evaluation.

What is leadership?

Discussion

(1) List all the qualities you would look for in a potential manager or supervisor. Reduce the list to a short list of 15 and rank these in order of priority.
(2) Is it possible to state categorically what qualities are necessary to be a good leader?
(3) Would anyone possessing the qualities you have listed automatically make a good leader?

(4) If all these qualities are necessary, does this mean that it is not possible to train people to lead? Must they be born leaders?

Perhaps it is not so much the qualities someone possesses, but their knowledge and ability to do the jobs of those under them which counts. It has been said that 'Authority flows from the one who knows.' But does it? A brilliant chemist may be promoted to be a manager: often the consequence of this is the loss of a highly trained technologist without a gain in management expertise. Another theory of leadership suggests that anyone put in charge of others can improve his performance by

- Ensuring the required tasks are continually achieved
- Building and reinforcing the needs of the group for team-work and team-spirit
- Meeting the needs of each individual member of the group for self-fulfilment.

The leadership model illustrated below shows how these three areas interact.

If the leader concentrates only on the task in hand — for example going all out for production schedules while neglecting the training, encouragement and motivation of his team and individuals — he may do very well in the short term. Eventually, however, those people will give him less effort than they are capable of. Similarly, a leader who concentrates only on creating team spirit while neglecting the task and the individuals will not get the full contribution from his people. They may enjoy working in his team but will lack the real sense of achievement which comes from accomplishing a task to the limits of one's ability. To be a good leader one must pay attention to all three areas.

Conclusion

So we come to the conclusion that, as is so often the case in industry, the answer to the question 'What makes a good leader?' is not straightforward. People with certain qualities are more likely to make effective leaders than others. At the same time it is undoubtedly necessary for a manager or supervisor to have the technical competence required by the task. But these alone are not enough. A leader needs to keep in mind the needs of the task, team and individuals, and if he can balance these, he will probably be a successful manager.

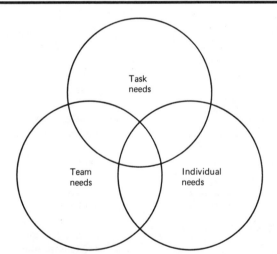

Task needs
The difference between a team and a random crowd is that a team — for example a football team — has some common purpose or goal. If a working team does not achieve the required result it will become demoralised. Organisations have a task: to make a profit, to provide a service, perhaps even to survive. So anyone who manages others within the organisation must achieve results; this is a major criterion of success.

Team needs
To achieve the desired results the group needs to be held together. People need to be working in a co-ordinated fashion in the same direction and proper team-work will ensure that the team's contribution is greater than the sum of its parts. Conflict within the team must be used effectively — arguments can lead either to ideas or to tension and lack of co-operation.

Individual needs
Within working groups individuals also have their own needs. They need to know what their responsibilities are, how they will be needed and how well they are performing. They need an opportunity to show their potential, assume responsibility and receive recognition for good work.

Class activity

It is possible to test how important effective leadership is by simulating a working group trying to achieve a task. The nature of the task is unimportant, the principles should still hold good. Here are two possible examples.

Jigsaw — simulation

Jigsaw is an alternative exercise taking less time and is organised in exactly the same way as Letterpoint.

Evaluation for the simulations

For both exercises above one of the observers from each group is called upon to make a brief assessment of how the group and its leader performed. Discuss these assessments. Pay particular attention to the following questions:

(1) Was the task achieved?
(2) Did the leader organise his groups satisfactorily?
(3) Were the team happy about their performance?
(4) Did the individuals feel they were being used to their full potential?
(5) Were the leaderless groups as effective as those with a leader?
(6) Were some of the groups more effective than others and, if so, was this related to the actions of their leaders?

The following case studies illustrate two aspects of management and supervision. The first shows that being the boss is not always as easy as it appears. The second describes a common dilemma for those in charge: 'Should I take time consulting everyone who might be involved in the consequences of a decision or wouldn't it be much easier, and quicker, just to go ahead and decide by myself?'

Letterpoint — simulation

The class is divided into groups of seven. Five of the seven make up the working group, and one of these five is the leader. The other two members act as observers. The leader is given a set of instructions which the group has to carry out. The observers are asked to watch the group in operation, and write down their observations on how the leader and the group performed.

You may also try having one group working without a leader, in which case each member would be given a copy of the brief. The observers would function in the same way as for the other groups.

Colin Miller's promotion — case study

The problem

At the Cape Insurance Company, at least two people have been worried for the last three months about the same thing: the situation in the accident department. The two people are *John Maddison*, administration manager of the branch office, and *Colin Miller*, recently appointed superintendent of the accident department, responsible to John Maddison.

Maddison cannot understand how it is that Miller, who was promoted six months ago, has not achieved what was expected of him: to keep output high and to run the department as a good working team. Did they make a mistake, he wonders, in promoting Miller. Yet it seemed logical enough at the time. Miller was a well-respected man in the office — the obvious choice for the job. They had given him the title of supervisor, two promising new juniors, and an office with a view of the department's room, so that he could keep an eye on things while he got on with his own work.

But what has happened? The section appears to be falling apart. Two of the staff have asked for transfers — and got them; time-keeping has been appalling and yet those in the department have been perpetually working overtime. And Miller is beginning to look like an old man.

Colin Miller is equally worried. He realises that he is failing in the new job. It seems to him that the situation is deteriorating daily. Yet, as far as he's concerned, he can honestly say that he has never worked harder in his life. If it were not for the extra salary, he would just as soon be back at his old desk alongside the other clerks. Promotion was all very well, but it didn't bring an extra eight hours in every day; only an extra eight hours' worry and responsibility.

He still has most of his old job of accident clerk to get through. In addition he now is responsible for managing the department — seeing that everyone is fully employed, pulling their weight, working together as a team. Two of his best chaps have left since he's taken over; he is sure that John Maddison blames him for that. And what about those who are getting slack and coming in late? Maddison has already dropped hints that something should be done about that. Yet it wasn't easy to reprimand Jones about his time-keeping when not only have you been sitting next to him for the past three years, but have had lunch with him nearly every day. In fact Jones has been getting slack for ages.

It was a pity he couldn't off-load some of his own work onto Jones. He'd transfer it like a shot if he thought Jones could be trusted with it, but he knew it would never work. Also what was he to do with the two new chaps in the department? They were both very promising and ought to be given the chance to do some more advanced work, but when would he have time to do all the replanning which this would entail? They would probably be the next to leave.

He imagined that there must be an answer to the whole problem, but he could see neither what it was nor how to solve it. Perhaps this management business wasn't so easy after all.

Discussion

(1) How do you think Colin Miller ever got into this state?
(2) Was Miller properly prepared for his promotion?
(3) What do you think Maddison should have done about this?
(4) Why do you think Maddison chose Miller for the new job?
(5) Was Miller really 'the obvious one for the job'?
(6) How would you have trained Miller for the job?
(7) How far do you blame Maddison for Miller's difficulties in fitting the work in, and how far do you blame Miller himself?
(8) Is it a good idea to promote someone to head of a department in which he has previously been on equal and friendly terms with those he is now expected to supervise?
(9) How do you think Miller can make time to deal with his new responsibilities?

(10) Is Miller's attitude right?
(11) What would you do to get him out of it?
(12) How could you prevent the same problem arising again?

Five foremen — case study

This case study illustrates some of the problems faced by managers and supervisors in making decisions.

The problem

Andrew Bannister, manager of Lichfield Plant Services, has been asked to send a foreman to visit the supplier of a new digger and discuss what extras Lichfield should order with it. Five foremen will be involved with the digger, and Andrew is undecided as to which one to send.

Henry is near to retirement but very competent and wouldn't let the firm down. It is unlikely that he would be pleased at the prospect of the trip which would mean not only travelling but also spending a night in a hotel.

Oliver has great potential and is ambitious, but he doesn't seem to get on well with the men and they might not accept his choice of the extra equipment.

Bob is very much one of the lads and a good foreman. He wouldn't have any trouble persuading the men to accept his choice. But, his language is terrible and the suppliers might be shocked if he didn't like what he saw and told them in no uncertain terms what they could do with it.

Dennis is a bit casual in his attitude to work and not keen on doing any extras, but he is steady and reliable and the men respect him. He is very active away from work, but doesn't seem to have that amount of interest in his job.

Herbert is very intelligent — quite an intellectual — but regarded as soft by the men, who do not respect him.

Discussion

(1) If you were Andrew Bannister, how would you decide which foreman to send?
(2) What approaches could you use to reach a decision? Of these which would be best?

What actually happened

Andrew decided there were four different ways in which he could make the decision. He could

- Decide by himself and then go and explain the decision to the foremen
- Talk to each foreman individually and then decide for himself
- Call the five foremen together and decide jointly
- Explain the problem to the five and let them decide amongst themselves.

He thought about the problem for a week and eventually made a decision completely on his own. He 'cheated' and sent two foremen: Oliver because he is competent and could be trusted to choose the right equipment and, in spite of the worry that the manufacturers might be offended, Bob because the men would accept the choice if they knew he had been involved.

The sequel

There were two sequels to the story. Dennis came to see Andrew; he was upset because he hadn't been chosen. 'Surely you know', he said, 'that I used to run a road-contract business and buying plant was part of my job. I sold out for £50 000, and I just come here for the pocket money and something to do.' Dennis would have been the ideal choice and the men would have respected his decision.

The other thing that happened was this. When the representative delivered the new digger he shouted to one of the men: 'Here it is then, your s . . . new digger, and I hope you b . . . well look after it!' Of course he was used to dealing with road construction people who are not renowned for genteel speech. He and his colleagues would never have been offended by Bob.

Discussion

Where did Andrew go wrong and what lessons can we learn from his mistakes?

Motivation and Money

10

Why do people go to work and what makes them work hard when they get there?

These are questions on which opinions differ greatly and extensive research has been carried out. If you were asked how to list the five most important reasons why a person works, undoubtedly somewhere in that list, probably at the top, would be money. But how important is money as a motivator? Does increasing a person's pay-cheque automatically increase his input to the job? Some people in industry believe it does, but others disagree.

Theory X and Theory Y

Douglas McGregor looked at the different approaches to motivating people and classified managers and supervisors according to their views. He called the two extreme attitudes Theory X and Theory Y (see table). He pointed out that in practice most people would come somewhere between the two, but under certain circumstances their behaviour could reflect attitudes consistent with both extremes.

Example: If you see a man putting his hand under a moving knife, you do not consult him before you knock his hand away. If you consulted first, he might admire your motivational thoughts, but he would have preferred to have retained his hand.

A Theory X manager would emphasise the need for close supervision, firm discipline and payment incentive schemes to counteract 'man's natural laziness and

Man's Attitude to Work

Theory X	Theory Y
Man dislikes work and will avoid it if he can.	Work is necessary to man's psychological growth.
	Man wants to be interested in his work and, under the right conditions he can enjoy it.
Man must be forced — or bribed — to put out the right effort.	Man will direct himself towards an accepted target.
Man would rather be directed than accept responsibility, which he avoids.	Man will seek, and accept, responsibility under the right conditions.
	The discipline a man imposes on himself is more effective, and can be more severe, than any imposed on him.
Man is motivated mainly by money.	Under the right conditions man is motivated by the desire to realise his own potential.
Man is motivated by anxiety about his security.	
Most men have little creativity — except when it comes to getting round management rules!	Creativity and ingenuity are widely distributed and grossly underused.

Source: D. McGregor, The Human Side of Enterprise (McGraw Hill, 1961).

```
                    Self-realisation
                    Growth
                    Personal development
                    Accomplishment
                    Talents fully used
                    Creativity

                Self-esteem
                Self respect
                Respect of others
                Autonomy/Responsibility
                Appreciation/Recognition
                Achievement
                Knowledge
                Status

            Social
            Sense of belonging  ⎫
            Giving friendship   ⎬ Love
            Receiving friendship⎪
            Social activities   ⎭

        Safety
        Protection from danger, threat, deprivation
        Security

    Physiological
    Food, drink, air, warmth, sleep
    Shelter
```

Source: After A. H. Maslow.

irresponsibility'. A Theory Y manager would see work as potentially satisfying in itself and seek opportunities for delegation, job enrichment and participation. In general leaders in any walk of life tend to move further towards the Theory X carrot-and-stick approach when under pressure. In more relaxed times they will incline to take the more positive view of human nature.

The hierarchy of needs

In order to increase the commitment of people to their work, today's companies have to be very much aware of their employees' needs, and the relative importance of these needs. Behavioural scientist Abraham Maslow developed a hierarchy of needs to explain motivation which he depicted in the pyramid reproduced above.

At the bottom of the pyramid are the needs of our animal nature for self-preservation. These needs are basic (as someone aptly said — 'man does not live by bread alone, except when there is no bread') and once satisfied, they cease to be strong motivators. Thus, as man begins to feel more materially secure, his higher needs for self-expression (including the drive for achievement), for an objective and for self-fulfilment clamour for satisfaction.

It follows that man can be self-motivated, and the task of the manager is to create conditions of work in which this will take place. In situations where this is difficult to achieve, as in dull, repetitive work, higher pay remains of paramount importance because workers are forced to find satisfaction outside their work.

Satisfaction and dissatisfaction

Research carried out by Frederick Herzberg sheds further light on the subject. He asked many people in different jobs at different levels two questions: what factors lead you to experience extreme dissatisfaction with your job and what factors lead you to experience extreme satisfaction with your job?

He collated the answers and displayed them in the form of the chart below, showing the order and frequency in which factors appeared.

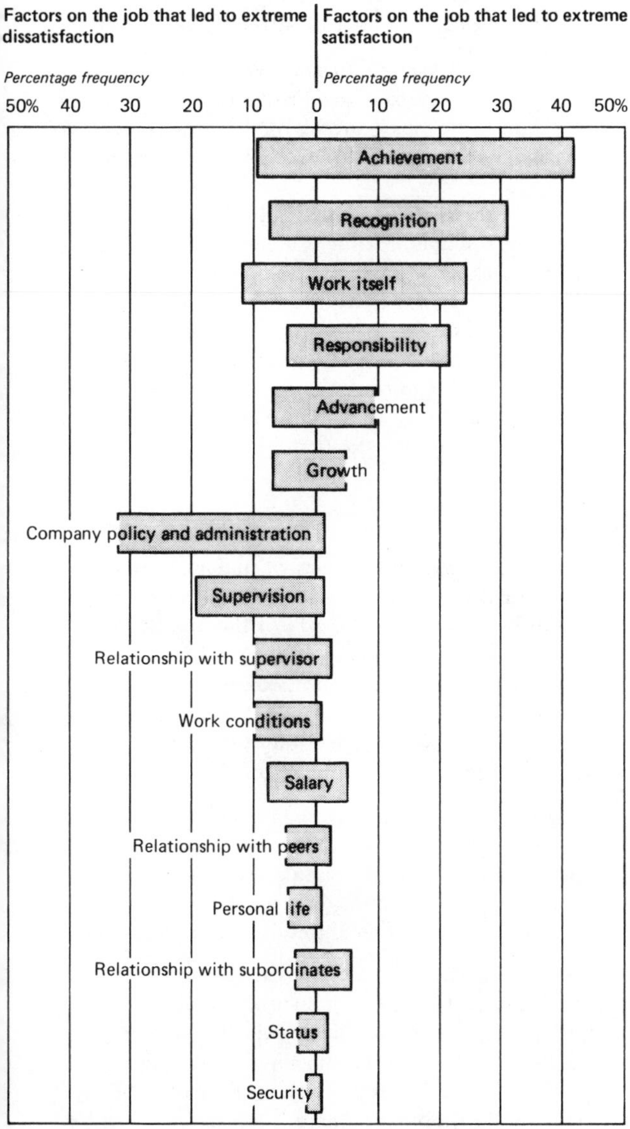

Herzberg suggests that the factors on the left-hand side of the chart can make people very dissatisfied, but do not positively motivate them to work harder. He calls them 'hygiene factors' and says that by giving more of them 'you just remove unhappiness, you don't make people happy'. These factors match the bottom three levels of Maslow's hierarchy.

If organisations fail to provide adequate 'hygiene factors', people tend to be very dissatisfied, but however adequate such things as salaries and fringe benefits are, they do not by themselves inspire people to give of their best.

Factors on the right-hand side of the chart have little to do with money and status and much to do with achievement and responsibility. They match the top two levels of Maslow's hierarchy and are connected with job content. Herzberg calls them 'motivators'. It is these that seem to play a vital role in increasing people's commitment to their work and their company.

Factors on the job that led to extreme dissatisfaction | Factors on the job that led to extreme satisfaction

Percentage frequency | Percentage frequency

50% 40   30   20   10   0   10   20   30   40   50%

- Achievement
- Recognition
- Work itself
- Responsibility
- Advancement
- Growth
- Company policy and administration
- Supervision
- Relationship with supervisor
- Work conditions
- Salary
- Relationship with peers
- Personal life
- Relationship with subordinates
- Status
- Security

Source: Frederick Herzberg, Work and the Nature of Man.

Motivation in practice

Obviously these theories do not lay down hard and fast rules, but they do give useful guidelines. They focus attention on the vital importance of factors such as

- Good supervision which encourages and extends rather than restricts
- Job satisfaction, which can often be increased through work restructuring and job enrichment programmes
- Team work
- The setting and achieving of targets with recognition for work well done.

The relative importance of the various factors is likely to vary from person to person, circumstance to circumstance and job to job. It may change with age, education and position with the organisation. Firms need to be aware of the basic necessary 'hygiene' requirements and to strive to increase the likely 'motivators' in the **working environment wherever possible.**

Discussion

(1) From your experience of human nature would you incline towards the Theory X or Theory Y approach to management? If your attitude is somewhere between the two, try to pinpoint it on a scale of 1–10, 1 being Theory X and 10 being Theory Y. What problems are likely to be faced by a manager who adheres closely to one or other extreme?

(2) Ask any students who have had any work experience through, perhaps, holiday jobs the question: 'What factors during your time at work caused you either extreme satisfaction or dissatisfaction?' Alternatively this question could be asked of a sample of people who work outside school. From the results build up a simplified Herzberg diagram and see how this compared with the figure on page 77.

(3) What would you consider to be the relative importance of the various hygiene and motivating factors for a person in each of the following jobs:

- A production line worker
- A senior manager
- A secretary
- A first-line supervisor
- A lorry driver?

(4) Of the following factors, which do you think you would regard as most important when considering a career yourself? Rank them in order of priority 1–12.

- Level of achievement
- Possibilities of promotion
- Job interest
- Personal relationships with supervisors and managers
- Personal relationships with colleagues
- Personal life outside work
- Recognition for effective work
- Responsibility
- Salary
- Security
- Status
- Physical working conditions.

Making the job more worthwhile

If we accept that money is not the only factor which attracts people to work, we should look more closely at the possibility of making jobs more rewarding when they get there. We have stressed the importance of the attitude and behaviour of the 'boss' in increasing commitment, but what about improvements to the job itself?

Many jobs are boring, monotonous and repetitive, and it is sometimes difficult to see how this can be remedied at a reasonable cost. However, companies can often arrange jobs in a way which at least makes them less bad, if not particularly satisfying. Here are some examples.

Job rotation

In years gone by a good deal was done on job rotation, in which each person in the team would move from one job to another. Such rotation is resisted by people who want to settle down to one particular job. However, it may help relieve the monotony if the supervisor gets each member of his team to do the others' jobs. Job rotation will only increase involvement marginally, because it means doing a succession of jobs, each equally repetitive.

Longer job cycles

A better solution is to organise the operation so that each operator has a number of different things to do.

Example: A vacuum cleaner was originally constructed by operators on a production belt carrying out short cycle jobs — such as one operator repeatedly putting a nut on a bolt of each sweeper as it passed him by.

When the same company came to make a floor polisher, the operator sat at a bench and trays of the various parts making up the polisher revolved round him. He was therefore able to build up a complete polisher step by step and put his number on it. The repetition was a longer cycle and he could take some pride in the end product.

The second way of organising the job was a good deal less boring than the first.

Job enrichment

The third, and even better, way of making jobs more worthwhile is not by increasing the variety of similar jobs, but by enriching the depth of the job. Each person is encouraged to take decisions about how he will do his job. He is involved in discussions before the leader takes a decision on behalf of the group. He may carry out his own inspection of the job rather than this being done by an inspector.

Example: In an aircraft engine repair unit, the supervisor of each small team was trained and qualified as an inspector and carried out the inspection of his own production instead of the normal method of having a separate inspection department.

The leader who delegates a great part of his job to his secretary and lets her get on with it, rather than acting as a dictating machine or using her as a copy typist, will not only get through a great deal more work but will make the secretary's job more worthwhile.

This form of job enrichment is largely achieved by delegating many of the decisions about the job to a lower level. Work is more rewarding if people are able to take their own decisions and are accountable for the results.

Reorganising jobs to make them more worthwhile is not always straightforward and can often be a slow and painstaking process. However, examples of its success in industry both in Britain and abroad illustrate the way this concept can be developed in future. Also, the introduction of new technology may mean that many of the more boring tasks can be carried out by machines rather than men.

The following examples of job restructuring in practice were discovered by John Bailey, head of the Management and Training Advisory Centre and principal lecturer and consultant in management and organisation in the Regional Management Centre at Bristol Polytechnic, in a recent investigation into the subject.

Moulding work to people

John Bailey

Recently I was lucky enough to obtain a study grant from the International Council for the Quality of Working Life to look at what people have been doing in the field of work restructuring. Having worked for a number of years in industry and more recently acted as a consultant for a number of firms, I still feel we have not yet found the answer to gaining people's involvement and commitment at work.

I visited about 15 companies in the U.K., Denmark, Holland and Belgium who have successfully introduced changes but not necessarily publicised them to a high degree. The following examples illustrate the wide variety of the changes made but also indicate the advantages of work restructuring.

Maintenance workers at Philips — Copenhagen

A lot of dissatisfaction existed within the maintenance department and with the service it provided. The work was allocated by the foreman, which often resulted in difficulties. The men were not always interested in the work they were given and consequently worked slowly, even hiding from the foreman to avoid getting more jobs. By forming a group and allowing the men to allocate the jobs themselves most of these problems have been resolved. When a team has finished they look for the next job on the foreman's desk and he now acts mainly as a consultant. Since making this change, complaints have fallen to zero and the men even asked for clocking to be abolished so that they could go to any urgent jobs notified to the porter as they come into work.

United Biscuits — Liverpool

Managers often feel that they cannot apply job enrichment because of their technology. When the company first tried to introduce this type of change they found the opportunity for physical changes in the content of people's jobs very limited. Subsequently the emphasis was put on forming working groups recognising flexibility within each group and involving the employees through group meetings in issues such as safety, hygiene, costs, quality and control information. Whereas originally there was a supervisor for mixing, machinery and packing there is one manager in charge of the whole line and he can be responsible for two or three plants. The groups enjoy quite a high level of discretion, taking complete responsibility for task allocation, job rotation, working hours and quality. They would not, however, accept responsibility for discipline, saying they would not have kangaroo courts. Nonetheless, results showed less time lost in disputes, a reduction in employee turnover, and perhaps the greatest benefit, employees accept responsibility for their own behaviour and flexibility and the introduction of change is made easier.

Plumrose Meats — Denmark

At Plumrose they decided to try out more group orientated methods of management as opposed to the traditional management style of a family firm. The main changes in work restructuring were in the ham-cutting section where it was felt that working conditions were not very satisfactory with a long line layout and short cycle times. Section meetings were held every two weeks in which discussions about the changes and improvements that were possible took place. Six out of 42 ham cutters participated and as a result they agreed to form smaller groups of six to eight people. The idea spread through the whole section and they ended up with five small groups and a co-ordinator who meets a representative from each group. The results were a 15 per cent increase in throughput in the section. A questionnaire survey of employees indicated a favourable response and an interest in making further changes.

Female assemblers Philips — U.K.

Progress in work restructuring is by no means largely confined to Europe. One of the most comprehensive programmes has been at one of the smaller Philips factories in the U.K. Here, with the help of consultants, a factory employing 300 women assembling miniature valves progressively moved over to what they described as 'team-work' over a period of 2½ years. Here the initial interest of operators was achieved by involving them in choosing a new colour scheme for the factory. Gradually their ideas were sought for ways in which problems of absenteeism could be reduced. Their comments included, for example: 'If only I could plan my week as I want it, instead of coping with the daily fluctuations imposed on me by my foreman,' 'If only I could be trained to do some other job, I could then move around,' and 'If only I had more say in the acceptance or non-acceptance of components for my valves.' With the aid of training and help from supervisors, teams developed a high degree of discretion and autonomy including quality, monitoring output, aspects of administration and training.

Salesmen, Esso — Belgium

Opportunities and needs for work restructuring are not confined to the shopfloor. Here the object was to change the salesman's job from a functional order-taker to a profit-orientated salesman managing his own business. Previously the salesman had very little discretion. He knew little of his customer's business situation and had to refer to head office for all information and decisions regarding costs, prices and conditions. The main emphasis was on increasing turnover of oil sales which was not necessarily consistent with increasing profit. Fundamental changes were made where the salesman was given price discretion, and his performance was now evaluated on contribution to profit rather than turnover. To aid him in the process, major changes were made in the provision of information with the creation of a computer based 'data bank' which gave the salesman ready information, e.g. the name of the dealer; number of pumps; contract information; fixed and current assets; details of Esso investment; information on increases in volume and prices; costs of marketing, direct and indirect costs to point of sale; product costs; return on investment at point of sale. All this decreased the amount of time spent on non-productive administration and record keeping. A training programme helped them understand the new system and after a while they started selling tyres and batteries as well as oil and petrol.

Paper Processing — U.S.A.

The experience of one company in the U.S.A. bears out the need for adequate preparation and planning for change. One firm attempted to introduce autonomous group working covering the total production system, including converting warehouse and support functions. They tried to combine the flexibility of groups with a career structure for individuals. However, having introduced the change over a period of three months, conflict developed between group and individual needs for advancement and there was a reaction leading to the reinstatement of management and more direct control. Thus, moving too far too fast may have killed the possibility of this type of change for the future.

Summary

That work restructuring can give significant benefits both in terms of increasing involvement and productivity is evident from the survey and the examples quoted. The development of group working tends to lead to a flatter and more flexible organisation structure with improved motivation and involvement by group members in their task. It can also lead to improved quality labour utilisation, reduced absenteeism and employee turnover. While output is not necessarily higher than with traditional forms of organisation, productivity measured in input/output terms improves.

It is important to stress that this type of change should not be undertaken lightly. Work restructuring can take many different forms and it is essential that the approach is evolved by the people concerned as a result of careful diagnosis of the existing situation and of the alternative means and opportunities available. Changes at the level of the employee or work group can also have a significant impact on other parts of the system. There are implications for the role of supervision and service functions, on wage structures and information systems and for the style of management required. Acceptance of responsibility and increased involvement of employees is as much a function of the environment in which people operate as of the knowledge, skills and attitudes of work people themselves.

Source: Industrial Society, May/June 1978

Discussion

How might the job be made more rewarding for the following people?

- A canteen cook
- A railway ticket collector
- A shop assistant
- A panel beater
- A bank clerk
- An insurance salesman.

Class activity

The following case studies deal with two aspects of motivation, the first with job restructuring in a manufacturing company and the second with the role of the supervisor in improving the performance of a sales team.

Adams and Frazer — case study

The situation

Roger Crawford, recently appointed general manager of the shoemaking company Adams and Frazer, was determined to raise productivity and put the company ahead of its competitors. He brought in outside consultants who recommended the following steps:

- Improving administration procedures
- Improving facilities for employees, for example the canteen
- Negotiating a productivity payment incentive scheme with the unions.

The recommendations were carred out; Crawford waited for the anticipated improvement in performance. But he was to be disappointed. Labour turnover continued to be high and productivity showed no marked increase.

He discussed the problem with the personnel manager, Bill Clement, who felt Crawford was on the wrong track.

'More and more companies are discovering that higher wages, good working conditions and payment schemes are not persuading people to work more effectively. Without these things people may refuse to work or look for new jobs, but the motivation to work effectively seems to come from satisfaction from the job itself.'

Crawford and Clement decided that it was management's responsibility to discover how people might receive more satisfaction from their jobs, and by doing so they would help the company as a whole. They called a meeting of all the heads of department to discuss how they should go about it. Some of the managers were sceptical: 'The only thing people work for these days is money' was the view they expressed. However, pilot schemes for the factory and the accounts department were agreed.

The factory

The factory manager and personnel manager worked out a scheme with the foremen in the plant. They then assembled the employees involved and explained their plan.

'The company has not been doing as well as management thinks it could in spite of all the recent improvements to conditions. We have therefore decided to try to approach the problem by re-organising jobs so that people can work more freely, and the supervisors and managers can manage more effectively.'

The essence of the plan was to

- Divide the labour force into groups headed by a team leader who would be responsible for the work of the group. This would leave the foremen more time for planning ahead and dealing with human problems.
- Make each team responsible for its own stocks and materials, with authority to reject parts coming to it from other sections which were below standard.
- Allow each team to inspect its own work, handle complaints from other sections about the quality of its work, organise its own job rotation, sickness and holiday replacement, and have some say in recruitment to the team.
- Consult teams on the design and method of assembly of the shoes and encourage them to try out any improvements to the job they could think of.
- Ask the team leader to give the team regular feedback on its targets and performance, which he would receive from the foreman.

Some people in the factory were against the experiment, saying that the shop floor did not want this type of

responsibility and it would just aggravate the situation. When at first productivity seemed to be declining rather than rising, there were a few smug faces about and an occasional 'I told you so' was heard.

However, the scheme quickly settled down and the workforce accepted it with enthusiasm. Productivity started to increase, and, more importantly, continued to do so.

The accounts department

In the accounts department the section chosen for the pilot scheme experiment dealt with purchase invoices. It was staffed entirely by women who did the same job every day. One checked the goods received by adding up columns on a small machine; another posted the goods received notes and produced documents which went to the cashier; another issued credit notes; and a fourth addressed the remittance advices and cheques on an addressing machine.

In the new scheme each woman was responsible for a group of suppliers. She checked whether the goods received were right or wrong, good or bad; she entered them into the purchase ledger, made up the traders' credits and addressed the remittance advices. In this way she would see the whole operation from start to finish and any errors would be her errors.

To the sceptics' surprise (certain people had been heard to mutter that it was a waste of time as women were more interested in their lunchtime shopping than the job anyway) once they became accustomed to their new jobs, the women liked the arrangement. The suppliers too found it better to deal with one person with their queries and would ask for her by name. Jobs were done more efficiently and in less time.

The result

Crawford and Clement were delighted with the success of the two experiments, particularly when they were able to announce to the employees that the company's share of the market had increased noticeably in the year since it started. They decided to extend the plan to other departments.

Discussion

(1) What were the essential elements in the changes that were made, and how did these contribute to job satisfaction?

(2) Could a similar method be applied to any type of job?

(3) Think of some jobs with which you are familiar. How might these principles be applied to these jobs and what sort of changes could be made to make them more interesting?

(4) Why do you think that this type of approach works?

Seedhill Chemical Company — case study

In this chapter and the preceding one we have said a lot about the importance of the supervisor in motivating people to work. In practice, however, it is not always as easy as it sounds. The following case deals with managing and motivating a sales team.

The problem

Seedhill Chemical Company manufactures a wide range of modern industrial chemicals. The business is highly profitable, but the company is not maintaining its share of an expanding market.

As far as can be judged, the company's products are fully competitive in both price and quality. The critical factor in the situation appears to be the sales representatives' efforts.

The sales director is concerned about this situation. He decides to take the opportunity — provided by ill health — to offer early retirement to the western area sales manager, who has been manager there for the past 12 years. To replace him he appoints Jim Robinson, aged 37 and with 10 years' service with the firm.

Robinson's last job was as distribution manager; before that he was a sales representative for five years.

Robinson has surveyed the work of the western sales office and talked to each of its 12 representatives. His conclusions so far are

- The older representatives seem to visit very few customers in a month; he notes that four out of the 12 are on their maximum salary.
- There is no agreed system for allocating new customers' telephone calls.
- Few new contacts are made or new accounts opened. There is a tendency to restrict visits to familiar customers.
- Most visits do not produce new business or useful information.
- During routine calls salesmen tend to deal only with items suggested by the office, and not to take advantage of new opportunities which arise.
- Most salesmen's visit reports are short and stereo-typed; the few longer reports are incoherent and full of irrelevancies.
- The procedure for handling and settling complaints appears unduly prolonged and this is causing some customer ill will and, on occasion, lost business.
- Sales representatives' salaries and conditions of employment are known to be better than average in the industry. They are not on commission.

Discussion

(1) What steps should Robinson take, or recommend, to improve the effectiveness of the department?

(2) Give your reasons for suggesting these steps.

Involvement: From Communication to Participation

One of the great debates of the 1970s was the way in which we should extend 'worker participation' in British industry. Strong and conflicting views have been expressed, but what is sometimes forgotten is what the objective of such participation really is.

The future success of our industry depends on achieving increased commitment of all its people to their work. Experience has shown that people are far more committed to implementing decisions when they have participated in their making. The more directly they are likely to be affected by the decision, the more this is so. The aim is to increase employees' involvement in the running of the departments and organisation in which they work.

The ways of achieving this involvement are not new but have been part of industrial relations for many years. Among these are three basic areas — communication, consultation and negotiation — which are essential to the process of participation and involvement.

Communication

Employees cannot be involved in making decisions if they do not know what is going on in the company

and why. Therefore, the first step is to make sure there is a good two-way flow of information through the organisation as illustrated below.

The most important roles in this communication chain are played by the managers and supervisors who pass information to the employees from management, often by calling them together regularly in what is

---

Management

Upward Communication

Methods
Managers walking the job
Suggestion schemes
Attitude surveys
Elected representatives

Information
Views, attitudes, fears, reactions, suggestions, proposals, dffficulties and aspirations of employees

Downward Communication

Methods
Written
— Company magazines
— Employee handbooks
— Annual reports
— Notice boards
Loudspeakers and closed circuit television
Face to face
— Mass meetings chaired by senior managers
— Supervisors talking to small groups

Information passed down
Decisions and proposals on company progress, performance, policies, movements of people etc.
Attitudes, ideas and feelings

Employee

known as a 'briefing group', and the employee representatives who report the employees' reactions back to management. (Further detail and a case study on communication from management is given in Chapter 8).

Consultation

The concept of joint consultation takes us a step further towards fully involving employees. In this way management can seek the views and advice of employees through their representatives before taking decisions on matters that affect them. When dealing with large numbers of employees, it is not usually possible to consult individuals, so consultation takes place at committee meetings where management delegates sit down with elected representatives. These are known as joint consultative meetings. They are held regularly and are formally constituted with a chairman, an agenda and minutes.

They are usually organised upon departmental lines, so that employees' valuable, specialised knowledge and experience can be used to improve effectiveness in their jobs. The departmental committees are then linked with a company committee where employee representatives meet top management. Where a company is unionised, trade union representatives usually serve on consultative committees. If only some of the employees of a company are members of trade unions the non-unionised employees elect representatives to these committees.

Negotiation

Negotiation also takes place between management and elected employee representatives, usually trade union representatives. In this case, however, a decision must be reached. Negotiation does not necessarily imply conflict over wages. Widening the scope of negotiations so that joint decisions are taken on policies under which management should operate can play a considerable part in building a feeling of involvement among employees.

Participation

Now let us look again at participation as a concept which not only embraces all three areas cited above but can go a stage further. In practice, participation and involvement may take place to a varying degree at four levels. These are

- At job level
- In management
- At board level
- In ownership.

Participation at job level

This is the level at which involvement is most real to employees. Here they can participate in decisions that directly affect their own jobs and method of working. Employee involvement is achieved by

- *Supervision* — where the supervisor looks after a small group, and involves them whenever possible in decisions which affect their work and in setting their own targets
- *Job design* — so that whenever possible a person has a whole job to do rather than a number of meaningless tasks and can take decisions on the ways he does the job
- *Communication* — making sure that each employee knows all that he needs to know to work effectively.

Participation in management

In order to participate at management level, employees must be told the background to the decisions facing management that affect them. Their respresentatives can then report their views to management through the joint consultation committees and take joint decisions through the negotiating channels.

Participation at board level

This is still only at an experimental stage in a few companies, and it is as yet unclear exactly what form boardroom participation should take. We have no widespread previous experience to point the way to success in this area, but there is evidence to suggest that representation of employees' interests at board level is a desirable goal. Most of this evidence comes from examples of participation abroad; few attempts have been made to introduce worker directors in this country.

Participation in ownership

This involves making the employees part-owners of the business or giving them shares in the profits. An important reservation is that it may not be in the employees' interest to have their life's savings and their life's work invested in the same enterprise.

The 'Fairfield Experiment' — an example*

This example illustrates employee involvement at work in the shipbuilding industry.

The 'Fairfield Experiment' was an experiment in participation which started at the Fairfield Shipyard in January 1966 and ended 27 months later when the yard merged into Upper Clyde Shipbuilders. The lessons which came out of it are as relevant today as they were then.

* After an Industrial Society booklet, 'The Fairfields Experiment' by Oliver Blanford

The experiment was the application of management common sense to a situation fraught with deep industrial relations problems in a bid to return a shipyard of century-old traditions to profitability. The acceptance of necessary change in the organisation of work, stores control and retraining, could not have been achieved without the involvement of employees at every level. Through this a new atmosphere of co-operation and trust gradually developed.

The story

One afternoon in August a cheerful crowd stood on the launching platform of Fairfield's shipyard and watched the then largest ship to be built on the Upper Clyde slide successfully into the water. The watchers included, for the first time in British history, a group representing of the workers who built the ship, invited by management.

Ten months before, the shipyard had been rescued from bankruptcy by the initiative and drive of Iain Stewart, chairman of Hall Thermotank. Stewart saw Fairfields as a proving ground to demonstrate that bankrupt yards could be turned into profitable enterprises if managed in an enlightened manner. In extremely unpromising circumstances, and with great determination, he and his new managing director Oliver Blanford gathered together a workforce, and a team of professional managers, none of whom were familiar with shipbuilding. Money for new investment came from the Government, various trade unions and private shareholders.

At a meeting of the entire staff of Fairfields in a cinema, Stewart called for a pledge of complete co-operation. The men promised to eliminate strikes, go-slows and overtime bans, to end demarcation and to co-operate in the modern techniques of job evaluation and work study, so that ships could be delivered on time and at a profit. In return Stewart promised to banish fears of unemployment, to establish union representation on the board and introduce regular, direct progress reports.

The problems

The new management started by looking at existing problems.

- Everywhere there was waste — waste of materials, waste of time and waste of manpower — of which the following are examples. The draughtsmen prepared drawings with excessive detail — even including 440 little stools in one ship's cocktail bar; there was

£25 000 of redundant stocks, including enough rivets to last 410 years; the cost of cable theft alone was £150−270 per week; and there was much abortive work — one plate for a hull was installed eight times. On the manpower side, timekeeping was very poor with 15 per cent late every day; absenteeism was 17 per cent; men reputed to be skilled failed to pass trade tests; and the rift between management and worker was deep and wide. As the men put it, 'You don't negotiate, you stand up and fight like men.'
- Working conditions were poor, especially the wash-rooms, lockers and canteens.
- There was a complete lack of planning and co-ordination of the various sub-assemblies of the ships.

The changes

The new management, in co-operation with the men, made the following changes:

- They introduced budgetary, quality and stores control.
- They started controlled programming of ship construction.
- They introduced manpower planning, which involved describing and evaluating jobs, cutting the workforce by 750, retraining, not replacing labourers who left and pay increases for those who stayed.
- They clarified the organisation structure and lines of authority.
- They defined the responsibility of the foremen as representatives of management to the men, whose job it was to see that the men gave their best to their work, while at the same time understanding the men's problems.
- They defined the role of the shop stewards as representatives of the men to management.
- They introduced a policy of 'nothing for nothing' whereby unions who negotiated for wage increases had to prove increased productivity, though this was not entirely successful in practice.
- They introduced a disciplinary procedure, a promotion policy and a redundancy policy.

The part played by participation

The new atmosphere of involvement played a major and essential part in gaining acceptance for these changes, many of which were controversial and not likely to be popular unless explained with care and satisfactory reasoning.

There were several elements in the participation structure.

A series of management advisory committees

- The Central Joint Council, consisting of one representative of each of the 13 unions having men employed at Fairfields and four members of management, was set up. It was to meet four times a year to discuss overall yard policy. Over 18 months these moved from being a collection of men with great suspicion of one another to become a most effective body. There were two turning points. On one occasion the Council settled a strike of apprentices, and on another, when a new trade union member suggested that a vote should be taken, the rest turned to him and said, 'We do not do that here — we discuss matters until we arrive at a consensus.'
- Three shop steward conveners started to attend the yard management committee. They were there as elected representatives, to know more about, and comment on, management plans and policies. They did not vote or wish to vote. They thus influenced but did not share management's decisions.
- Departmental advisory committees were established to provide the manager who had to make a decision with a wider field of experience and to enable those concerned to hear and contribute to discussion of the advantages and disadvantages of a proposed course of action.

Board representation

Two national trade union officials were put on the Board — one from the Amalgamated Union of Engineering Workers (AUEW) and one from the General Mine Workers' Union (GMWU).

Communication system

A communication system was set up which included

- Briefing groups for communication of management decisions down the line (a message could be passed to all 3500 workers in one hour)
- 'Fairfield News' for more general communication
- Regular meetings, conducted by the chairman and managing director, at six-month intervals for all staff
- 'The policy of 100 explanations', laid down by the managing director, whereby his managers were to go on explaining changes until they were understood
- Weekend conferences for managers and foremen.

Additional training

Training of shop stewards in work study, quality and production control as well as trade union matters was started. Nominated worker representatives attended courses in industrial engineering and its terminology so that they could explain the problems of men to management and vice versa.

The result

The decision by the Government to push the Fairfield yard into the Upper Clyde Shipbuilders merger in 1968 cut the experiment abruptly and prematurely short, but already an impressive picture was beginning to emerge

- Disputes over dismissals had disappeared
- Lateness and absenteeism had fallen by about 60 per cent
- Cost of cable theft had dropped to £25 a week
- Phasing out of demarcation with and between unions was being negotiated
- Three ships had been delivered on time
- The number of strikes had been cut by half

- Earnings were up
- New orders had been won
- There was an estimated small profit for the next financial year.

The following articles present two views, one from a trade unionist and one from a member of management, on the role of employee involvement in British industry. The first is by Ron Nethercott, regional secretary of the Transport and General Workers' Union (TGWU) Region 3, responsible for more than 150 000 members throughout the Southwest. He has been a trade union official for 30 years. The second is by Paul Blake, head of joint consultation administration at May & Baker Limited, an international company employing 5000 in the United Kingdom in the research, production and marketing of chemical products for the prevention of human, animal and plant diseases.

Employee involvement — the form this should take in British industry

Ron Nethercott

I always think we complicate the affairs of industry in respect of employer—employee relationships by creating too much mystique. People are beings, with emotions, fears, desires, hopes, in whatever situation — in their homes, in their leisure, in the places where they work.

We all know that a happy family life is based on communication with one another, and participating in and sharing common interests. Why, therefore, we have to complicate our relationships at work has always been beyond my understanding.

If people feel involved, and know they matter, of course they will respond. Belonging is a basic need of every human being. I am sure very often it is the remoteness of relationships in industry which causes problems.

Experience has taught me that communications are vital, and are generally good within well organised companies. However, I am mindful that communication is often lacking, particularly if you relate communications to paper and ink, and this is often the way that middle management (foremen and supervisors for example) have to make their thoughts and intentions known — not always with happy results.

To my mind, the spoken word is the best method of communication because, sooner or later, it leads to understanding. Sadly, we are often too busy to spend much time in communicating in this way, so maybe paper and ink is the only practical method in our society.

If we have to write to one another the message must be simple and to the point, but without brusqueness, so that people can understand and not be hurt or offended by what we are saying.

I know managing directors who find it difficult to interpret the financial affairs of their company because of the language of accountancy, which is a different language from that which most people understand. In fact our society is divided by this problem of words. So communication, I repeat, must be simple, understandable and truthful. We must avoid jargon at all costs.

Consultation must be regular, ongoing and personal. Unless this is so, joint decision-taking will be impossible, because if we reach the stage where a joint decision is necessary, and we are still thinking of 'them' and 'us', we have failed to achieve a basic understanding, and a 'joint' decision becomes a travesty.

We must beware of the trap of

thinking that because we have been talking to one another we are necessarily in harmony. The main purpose of communication is to bring people closer together, but if we just talk with no intention of seeing the other person's point of view, we are deceiving ourselves. We must make sure we all understand one another and come to a point of trust.

It is not the leaves of the tree which are important. They die during the autumn. It is the roots, set well in the ground, which weather the winter, and allow the tree to bud, flower and fruit.

The root of good industrial relations is belonging, and involvement through good communications.

Understanding makes us all work as a team. The achievement of a common goal obviates personal fears or jealousies because in good teamwork everyone has an essential part to play.

Involvement by joint consultation

Paul Blake

There are so many really urgent problems that are facing us. Problems of unemployment, galloping inflation, lack of investment — these are only some of the areas where we sometimes feel overwhelmed and need to grasp all the sources of help that are available to us. In industry, we have come increasingly to recognise the immensity of the contribution which employees can make, if only we will involve them. And in involving them we are only recognising the obvious fact that it is the people who are engaged in an enterprise who determine its success or failure.

Now it is a fact, also, that management must manage. Equally, employee representatives recognise areas where it is their duty to negotiate. But, in between those two areas, there is a third area which is neither managing, nor is it negotiating. Here there is a great list of subjects which can be explored jointly, management with employees. This is an area where the skills of employees, their special abilities, their special workingplace knowledge, can be harnessed to management's ability to organise and to finance. The result can only be for the good of both sides.

And here let it be said without any doubt that employees, no less than managers, will get their fair share of the rewards that arise from increased productivity or increased efficiency resulting from the fruits of consultation.

But it goes beyond that. Properly constituted — and that does not mean over-organised — joint consultation can lead to better understanding, better identification of needs and, above all, a better 'atmosphere'.

The quality of decisions made by management is improved immeasurably by adapting the knowledge and experience of those who are affected by the decisions; but not only that, it will lead to better co-operation in employing those decisions, because employees will accept unpopular decisions when their own opinions have been taken into account in a genuine way. Of course the unpopular decision must be accompanied by reasons why — this is part of the training aspect of joint consultation.

Also, joint consultation is a face-to-face relationship with either side listening to the other, without fear of recrimination, or misunderstood motives, or meanings that can be misinterpreted, as when put on paper.

It is management's job to take the initiative, but every good manager takes the views of his people into account before arriving at a decision. Joint consultation is really this procedure enlarged and organised. Mostly, management asks the questions and seeks the opinions of its employees (although of course the employees can consult management about certain matters that are vital to them), and, having asked, management listens and perhaps asks further questions, and listens again. In the process, misunderstandings are reduced, managers and employees can understand each other's views and objectives, and reasoned arguments are made and discussed and reviewed.

Of course, management will need to give serious consideration to everything that has been said at joint consultation. In present-day industry and commerce, decisions can seldom be made on the basis of just one set of considerations; other matters need to be borne in mind — the cost, perhaps the preparedness of a market, or whether this is the psychological moment to give effect to what has been discussed. It is, of course, quite wrong to expect any employee or shop steward to take on the responsibility which a manager bears, without the salary, the status, and other things that are appropriate to that responsibility. So involvement in joint consultation is really a matter of joint decision-making rather than joint decision-taking; management takes the decision and bears the responsibility.

Don't think that joint consultation is just an easy way out! It is a positive recognition that a valid contribution can be made by everyone in an enterprise, and involving people in this form of participation in industry means a great deal of work, a great deal of listening, and a great deal of talking (but to the point) at the 'sharp end'. But it's a shared process, drawing management and employees closely together for their common benefit. And it works . . . I've seen it.

Discussion

These articles, together with the information on the previous pages, should give you an idea of the options open to business. In practice the situation in different companies is as diverse as the companies themselves, both in degree and approach.

If you were the members of a committee set up to produce a guide for industry on what direction it should be taking to achieve maximum benefit from employee participation, what would your recommendation be? You might consider the following questions.

(1) At what level in an organisation will employee participation makes the greatest contribution to the effectiveness of the enterprise?
(2) What forms of participation offer the maximum benefit to the employees themselves?
(3) If a company wishes to implement a programme for employee participation, what steps should it take and in what order?

Class activity

Involvement — role play

Alternatively participation in an organisation might be looked at by means of a role play involving managers in the company. In this case the discussion involves five characters who occupy middle management positions in a department store in a town in the Midlands with a population of 150 000.

Background

The store manager has been asked by the firm's head office to conduct an experiment in employee participation at his store. He has decided to start by introducing a pilot scheme involving those who sell goods to the customers; he must present a plan of how this is to be carried out to the next senior management meeting. Unfortunately he has only just arrived back from an overseas trip and the meeting is tomorrow.

He asks the assistant store manager to discuss the matter with the managers of the various departments, each of which has about 15 people working in it, and come up with some suggestions on a practical and feasible scheme for introducing employee participation in their areas.

Characters

At the meeting are

> *Jean Marsh* — Assistant store manager
> *Charles West* — Manager of the furnishings department
> *Rosemary Ford* — Manager, clothing department
> *Marion Brook* — Manager, haberdashery and fancy goods
> *Stanley Field* — Manager, china and glassware.

Industrial Relations and the Trade Union Movement

12

If you stop someone in the street and ask them 'What do you think about trade unions?', the chances are that you will get an emotional response which is either strongly for or equally strongly against them. Unfortunately it is far less likely that you will get an *informed* response.

This book does not set out to paint a picture of trade unions as exemplary organisations filled with saintly individuals working for the good of mankind. Trade unions, like other organisations including management ones, are manned by ordinary people who make mistakes; their structures are often cumbersome, their communication sometimes poor; they do not always appear to practise what they preach; and they do not always seem as responsible and constructive as they might be.

Nevertheless, without the organisation of workers into collective, respresentative bodies it would be exceedingly difficult to operate our complex industrial society.

To see today's trade unionism in perspective it helps to look back to how it all began.

A brief historical perspective

The first major step in trade union development was the establishment in 1829 of the Agricultural Workers' Union in Birmingham. At this time agricultural workers were well paid in comparison with their industrial counterparts, but the slump of the 1830s led to the landowners reducing their wages from nine shillings a week to eight, and then seven.

At the village of Tolpuddle, under the leadership of George Loveless, the men got together to see how they might defend themselves against these cuts. After failing to reach agreement with their employers, they turned for advice to the Grand National Consolidated Trade Union, led by Robert Owen, on whose advice they formed their own union — the Friendly Society of Agricultural Labourers.

At this the local employers and magistrates took fright. They sought guidance from the Home Secretary, Lord Melbourne, and as a result George Loveless and five fellow labourers were arrested to set an example to the nation. In March 1834 they were sentenced to seven years' deportation under the Mutiny Act which forbade the taking of 'unlawful oaths'.

With the relief of the trade depression in the late 1840s trade unions became stronger financially, better organised and less local. In 1851 the Amalgamated Society of Engineers was formed, which served as a model for national union development for skilled workers. Particularly important was the new concept of the payment of 'friendly benefits' — financial assistance by the union for workers' families during sickness and unemployment.

In the 1860s trade unions started to co-operate with one another, first locally, for example in the London Trades Council, and then nationally, forming the Trades Union Congress in 1868.

In spite of this activity trade unions were not granted legal status until 1871 when a Royal Commission was set up which decided that membership of a trade union was not illegal. From this time on trade union recognition was far more widespread and local negotiating machinery with employers was established.

Towards the end of the nineteenth century trade unions became affiliated to the new independent parliamentary Labour party and the political levy was introduced.

The start of the First World War heralded the coming of a new figure to the industrial relations scene. Because all the full-time officials had been called up, shop stewards were appointed to represent the workers, a move which was encouraged by management since they were employees and therefore on the spot. The shop steward has been a key figure in our industrial relations system ever since.

After the war unemployment again rose. In 1926 there was the General Strike, which started with the mineworkers protesting at cuts in their wages. By the time of the General Strike there were about 5.25 million union members in Britain.

Once again there was a lull in trade union development during the Second World War, but in the 1950s the movement stabilised. At this time most people earned low basic wages which were made up by bonuses for piecework and overtime.

The 1960s witnessed extensive wild-cat striking. In 1964 another Royal Commission was established to look at trade unions and employer associations; this resulted in publication of the Donovan Report.

The main landmarks in trade unionism during the 1970s has been the passing of extensive legislation affecting both union and employer activities, and the co-operation of the unions with the Labour Government during the time of the Social Contract. The Conservatives passed the first Industrial Relations Act in 1971, which was later repealed by the Trade Union and Labour Relations Acts of 1974 and 1976. These extended the protection for employees, provided new freedoms relating to union membership, and legalised the closed shop once more. (Further detail on recent legislation can be found on page 116).

One of the main features of British trade union development is the formation of large numbers of unions on a so-called 'craft' basis — that is, each representing groups of workers in particular jobs, rather than all the workers in a single firm or industry. In 1972 there were 550 trade unions recognised in Britain, compared with only nine in West Germany where since the war they have been organised nationally on an industry-wide basis. This number is, however, decreasing slowly as unions merge for economic reasons. In 1972 there was a total of 3650 employer organisations.

Trade union membership has been growing steadily and spreading from the original groups of blue-collar workers into the white-collar areas of clerical and technical staff and, in some industries, supervisors and managers. This has followed a corresponding rise in the proportion of white-collar to blue-collar employees, a trend likely to continue. By 1976 the total membership of trade unions in Britain was over 12 million out of a total working population of about 25 million.

Trade unions today — their structure and role

Trade unions are structured bodies set up to represent their members, the employees. The key element in the role of a trade union is that the union is responsible to the employees it represents, not to management, the government or anyone else for that matter.

Trade unions are financed by regular contributions paid by all their members on the basis of a percentage of wages. This money is then invested. The income is used to pay for the administration of the union and the salaries of its full-time officials, to provide benefits for employees and to fund the TUC on a membership basis.

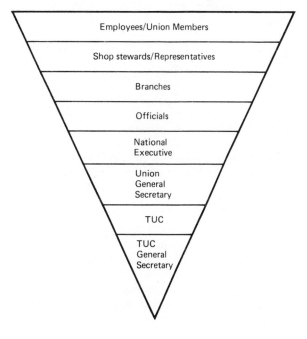

In addition there is a levy which members can pay if they so wish which is used for political purposes.

Trade unions are structured on the basis of an inverted pyramid, as shown in the figure on page 91. In contrast to the pyramid showing the management structure (page 65), the union and its officials do not manage the members but represent their views. The members own the union, not vice versa.

The union structure is made up of the following:

The *shop steward*   Union members at the workplace elect their own spokesman, usually known as the shop steward or representative, who is not paid for his union work and often carries on his normal job but is given time off for union activities. The steward speaks for union members on all problems that need to be dealt with on the spot, such as questions of safety and overtime arrangements. He also helps with individual problems such as clearing up misunderstandings on the details of their pay. He plays a major part in communicating employees' views to management and company-level negotiations.

The *union branch*   Union members belong to a branch often based in their local area, which meets regularly and where they can have a say in what the union does and how it is run. Each branch has an elected secretary, chairman and committee, and sends delegates to the union's annual national conference. Resolutions from the branches are transmitted to the conference and, if accepted, can become official union policy.

The *national organisation*   Each union has a national executive committee which acts on behalf of its membership. This is elected either at the national conference or by a ballot of members. Most unions also employ full-time paid officials who give advice and help to shop stewards and branches and represent the members in wage negotiations if required, usually at national level.

The *Trades Union Congress* (TUC)   The trade unions all come together in the TUC, one of whose many roles is to put forward a trade union point of view to the government on issues affecting trade union members. These might include legislation, economic and social service policies and facilities for employee training.

The trade union represents its members in the following areas:

* The negotiation of conditions of employment, including pay, hours, working conditions and fringe benefits
* In consultation with management on matters affecting their work such as organisation of jobs, planned expansions or closures

* In the grievance procedure by which an employee who feels himself wronged can take his problem up the management line with his representative to assist him
* In the discipline procedure
* At a national level, through the TUC
* In safety matters.

Where groups of employees are not unionised most of these functions are usually performed by some other representative body in the company, such as a staff association.

The following articles illustrate aspects of the relationship between employers and employees from various points of view.

The first, by George Arnold, divisional organiser of the Amalgamated Union of Engineering Workers (AUEW) in the Tyne district, takes a look at the joint actions employers and trade unions can take to improve this relationship. Mr Arnold is a toolmaker by trade who, before becoming a full-time union official, was a works convener.

Statistics have a tendency to be difficult to interpret and can often be misleading. Nevertheless they are sometimes all the information we have on which to base a judgement. In the second article Dan van der Vat, of *The Times*, looks at some figures on strikes in Britain and abroad.

The third is a transcript of a taped interview conducted by Rank Audio Industrial Services during research into material for managerial and supervisory training films. The interviewee had been a supervisor for only a short time, but had spent more than 20 years as a production worker. His success in putting into practice some of his ideas on management—employee relations at the workplace demonstrates the tremendous importance of the first-line supervisor in these relationships. This tape has been used widely over the past few years for training managers and supervisors.

Finally, there is the perhaps slightly tongue-in-cheek description of how strikes look from the factory floor written by J. J. Maling, a former shop steward and for 10 years a trade union branch secretary.

Improving industrial relations
George Arnold

It is hardly conceivable that anything new can be written about the United Kingdom industrial relations scene. Not only has the subject led the field as it were for a decade in our own national industrial news reporting, it becomes increasingly apparent that the international press takes more than just a passing interest in the way that managements and unions conduct themselves in industry in this country.

It was not until President Carter intervened in the American mineworkers' strike that we in this country knew that a national strike had been in operation in the U.S.A. for at least three months. The same was the position in Western Germany with the metal industries in prolonged dispute, and as it was indeed in French and Italian industry with major national disputes. News about industrial disputes seems to travel more easily and explicitly from these shores to Europe and elsewhere than news of similar disputes in return. Frequent reference by our foreign industrial competitors to the so called 'British disease' conjures a picture of deplorable worker irresponsibility. The fact that the number of working days lost by industrial action in this country is nowhere near as many as are lost in the majority of other major industrial nations through strikes goes without mention.

For us to gloss over our industrial relations problems and to pretend that they are not there would be irresponsible and dishonest. We managements and unions have a joint responsibility to manage industrial relations and, of course, industry, much better than we have in the past if we are to benefit at all from the slow movement out of world trade recession, and if we are to grasp advantage from industrial growth arising from an adjusted economy and the benefits of North Sea oil.

Differentials difficulties
The Government also has a very important additional part to play. Not all Government industrial legislation or Government industrial policies have been helpful in our problems over the last three and a half years. For instance, while the three stages of pay policy since 1975 have gone a very long way towards correcting the inflationary trends, they have produced problems in respect to wage differentials that appear to be insoluble and will continue to have repercussions. These problems exist not only between the skilled and unskilled employees but also within the skilled and unskilled groups themselves.

Positive Government guidelines in this further aspect of pay policy might have alleviated the situation. It would seem, however, that nothing short of a complete reappraisal of local and national wage structures is needed to properly tackle the problem. When a new company is setting up in business in Development Areas the development corporation, local authorities and others, responsible for attracting new industry, will do everything possible to secure such industry for their local areas, but they seldom introduce the new employer to the appropriate trade unions or the relevant National Agreements. It is generally only after months of operation that the employees in the new company realise that they are being paid in one way or another less than the national agreement. The trade union then becomes involved with the employer for the first time, and unfortunately, not in the best of circumstances. If, before the company began its operation the management were able to meet the appropriate union officials to discuss the kind of agreements under which the company wanted to operate, very many problems which have produced disputes in new companies would never have arisen at all.

The trade unions have a great deal to concern themselves with in putting their own house in order. The combination of unions with like interests to speak as if with one voice in representation of the joint membership is an asset and attractive to the potential employer in the regions. But amalgamations are much easier to talk about than they are to achieve. Confederation works best at shop floor level.

When the recognised procedures are side-stepped and industrial action occurs, it is very often because the members know that the full-time trade union officer cannot be speedily available. This problem can only really be overcome if the number of trade union officials are considerably increased and this means increased trade union contributions which the membership not unnaturally are loath to accept. There is no doubt though, that as things are, the trade union official has far too much to do. He cannot be a specialist in every industry in which his members are employed. The quality of representation would be much better if local officials were always able to concentrate on only single industries. Alas, that cannot be the case in the trade union world just now.

There is no doubt that a revival of the demand for amalgamation from shop floor level and determination to succeed could bring about the means by which trade unions could represent with much greater efficiency and effectiveness. This development in itself could to a tremendous extent improve our industrial relations position.

Source: Industrial Society, July/ August 1978.

Strikes: are we really as bad as we think?
Dan van der Vat

The two industrial disputes at Birmingham and Bathgate which have cast another serious doubt over British Leyland's future will only confirm the belief of a legion of observers at home and abroad that 'the British are always on strike'.

BL's latest industrial relations disaster is a classic case. The British are on strike *again*. It is their motor industry *again*.

It is British Leyland *again*. It is the toolmakers (in one case) *again*. It is unofficial *again*. It is about pay parity *again*.

The word 'strike', its derivatives and its synonyms once more dominate the headlines. There could hardly be a better time to consider whether Britain deserves its reputation.

The seeker after truth who sets out to find an explanation for the British strike syndrome, if such it is, faces an extraordinarily nebulous assignment. Generalisations abound but patterns are all but impossible to discern. It soon becomes clear that there are lies, damned lies, statistics and strike figures. Theories are more plentiful than facts, and the most consistent and easily identified sound to be heard is the muffled beat of logic being chopped. There is a case (albeit not a strong one) for saying that a layman interested in looking for reason in British industrial relations would be well advised to find something more constructive to occupy his time.

For the record, my researches took me from the industrial relations summit at Warwick University (which has a reputation second to none) to the TUC, from the CBI to ACAS (the Advisory, Conciliation and Arbitration Service) and the Institute of Personnel Management.

Further comfort in this lonely task was provided by years of intermittent reporting of many kinds of industrial dispute and considerable first-hand knowledge of labour relations in West Germany, constantly (and, I fear, wrongly) held up as an example to us all.

The first conclusion the undaunted observer is obliged to reach is that the British are obsessed by strikes, rather as the West Germans are obsessed by inflation. One of the great British folk-memories of this century is the General Strike of 1926, perhaps because it happened only nine years after the Russian Revolution. The workers involved in it amounted to only about one-seventh of the number of French strikers who brought their country to a standstill for weeks in the summer of 1968 — but the French are not obsessed by strikes.

Rightly or wrongly, but certainly faithfully reflecting the level of public interest, British newspapers, radio and television devote enormous amounts of space and time to strikes.

Since the principal media are national rather than regional, a strike in Caithness is common gossip in Cornwall, and it is all too easy for foreign correspondents to report British strikes abroad. It is for this reason, presumably, that Mr Kenneth Graham, assistant general secretary of the TUC, usually finds, as he told me, that visiting North American trade unionists are better informed about the latest British strike than they are about a quite savage and protracted dispute in Canada or the United States. An American labour relations expert told me: 'A Californian just doesn't want to know about a Pittsburgh steel strike.'

Mr James Mortimer, chairman of ACAS, pointed out that it is the period between the wars, from which the generally inaccurate public conception of the nature of strikes still largely derives, that was the departure from the norm, not the present. Then, wage cuts produced a series of confrontations between capital and labour on a national scale unknown before or since. Nowadays a nationwide strike is an extreme rarity. Where it occurs, it is almost always in a nationalised industry where the government or a state agency is the sole employer.

The accompanying table, which I compiled from the latest statistics published by the International Labour Organisation (ILO), a United Nations agency, reveals almost as much as it conceals. Strike figures must be treated with caution. Many stoppages are not counted because they involve only very few workers or do not last a full working day, or simply because they are not

reported. Thus the traditional West German wage-bargaining tactic, the warning strike of a few hours or less, perhaps involving hundreds of thousands of workers, does not appear in the figures at all.

Nor is any one year typical, and comparisons between countries are always traps for the unwary. For Britain, 1976 was a comparatively trouble-free year. Last year was worse, and 1978 is already much worse still. The Italian figures reflect the local custom whereby millions of workers award the nation an extra public holiday by striking for 24 hours, something the French do too, though on a smaller scale. A close study of such figures over a period of years does however permit one clear conclusion: that the British, when it comes to strikes, have nothing to boast about but also are nothing like as bad as they (and many foreigners) like to think.

Insofar as our reputation for striking is undeserved — because it is at variance with the facts — it can only be our own fault. Even in a bad year for strikes, we lose rather more working days through industrial accidents, 10 to 20 times more through sickness and 20 to 40 times more through that great unsung curse on industry, absenteeism. There is no ground for complacency in these comparisons, however, because they overlook the uniquely disruptive effect of strikes, which the present extreme examples at British Leyland show.

While it is difficult (if not impossible) and dangerous to generalise about strikes, they are invariably based on a grievance which is real to the strikers and invariably

Strikes in 1976

Country	Population m	Labour force m	Number of disputes m	Workers involved m	Days Lost m
Canada	21.6	8.8	1039	1.57	10.8
U.S.A.	214.6	96.9	5649	2.41	38.0
Japan	112.8	53.8	2720	1.36	3.3
France	52.8	22.1	4348	3.81	5.0
West Germany	61.5	26.7	(n/a)	0.17	0.53
Italy	55.3	19.6	2706	11.90	25.4
Australia	12.8	5.3	2055	2.19	3.8
U.K.	55.5	25.7	2016	0.67	3.3

Source: ILO.

occur after a breakdown in communication between management and workers. They are almost always local, small and of short duration and, despite all the publicity, *they usually come as a shock to both sides.* Pay is the usual visible issue, but there is overwhelming evidence that the British worker attaches more importance to the way he is treated than to his pay. Boredom, lack of consultation,

unfair dismissal, fear of redundancy and even of change, bad working conditions, outmoded union organisation, managerial remoteness in large companies and government policy are all far more important than is usually admitted.

They are also far more important as causes of strikes than agitation and bloody mindedness which, though they exist, are nothing like as common as

many people would like to think. Fast and flexible response at the workplace based on good communications is widely held to be the only answer to disputes. Striking is not the British disease, but only a symptom. Low productivity and low investment constitute the real bane of British industry.

Source: *The Times,* 1 September 1978.

From cabbage to human — an unedited recording of a comment by a new supervisor

I've worked in factories now for many years, certainly over 20, and I have yet to see a new starter walk into the factory on his first day or first week, determined to do as little as possible, as badly as possible for as much as possible. They choose to work at that factory, they want to work at that factory, and they want to do well, and I can see that factory change them in all too short a time, and I believe that it isn't necessary. I believe that that spirit that they come into the factory with can be bolstered, can be buttressed and can last them all their working life. If management will only recognise the need to do this and would only find the means. First of all they talk of the monotony of the job, you know, this changing of jobs that they're suggesting. It's not going to be the long-term answer. But fancy this, you're packed together in your working environment, working at the dictates of a machine — you may not go to the toilet, you may not back off — you know without your costing production — you're totally . . . you know it's worse than acting like a robot, because the robot is controlling you.

Right, you're stuck there eight hours a day, ten hours a night with the same faces. You can't choose the people you work with, you can choose your friends, you can choose your wife, but throughout the working week, you're seeing more of that chap and the people packed in around you, whether they be compatible, incompatible, whatever they are, you see more of him than your own wife, or your own friends, or your own children. You're in that atmosphere, you've done a repetitive thing. On my particular track, it's quite a long cycle. You go five minutes before you do exactly the same thing again. Now that's pretty good in

today's factories. Some of them have got a twenty second, ten second cycle. And there it is. And these people have the choice of becoming cabbages, right, or utilising everything that comes along.

A fellow would rather pick a fight with his foreman and create an issue than go unnoticed, or unrecognised. Just for the novelty of it. You find that these issues blow up over the silliest, most stupid little things. And it is purely and simply that they want a break from the tedium, from the repetitiveness because there's nothing there, there's nothing at the end of it.

And this is a prime concern of mine . . . . O.K. now instead of going to Blackpool for a week, they fly to Majorca for a fortnight. Many have got their colour televisions and instead of coming on a bicycle they come in a car. But that only makes the contrast between the outside life and the inside life sharper . . . and they need to be Jekylls and Hydes or go bloody mad . . . they've got to be schizophrenic . . . .

What's needed in Britain's factories today isn't a change of wage structures, it's not a change of procedures or a change between union leaders and the Engineers Employers Federation — it's a change in attitude to recognise that we owe these men something besides their wages.

These people are giving their lives to that company, and have at least as much right as the shareholders as to the future of that company . . . . I've got lads here who've put in 40, 50 years of their life. You tell me how to recover one day of that if this company doesn't treat them right. So I would insist upon at least consultation, try to get a feeling that these people are part of the company, not a necessary appendage to it. Now

management's responsibility is that they themselves must set the examples. They must treat their subordinates as if they care. They must include them in their decisions and let them know what they are looking for . . . they must decide as a matter of policy it is their responsibility, these people, these check numbers as they are . . . these production units as they are. Now they must recognise them — they've got heads, eyes, arms, legs. They're human beings with human needs and greeds and everything else that goes with it.

The answer is in training. I've always believed that they should select people and train people how to treat people. You know, it's no good making a machinist a foreman because he's a good machinist. He may be great moulding machinery, but how does he go about moulding men?

I think it's certainly a necessary ingredient to care about people. I think this is most necessary because if you don't care you'll never go to the trouble to find out what makes the other fellow tick and this is what's necessary to get to know the men as individuals.

To put pride into these people, they are full of pride outside . . . everybody has got something to be proud of . . . you know even if it's only having the longest hair in the street. Everyone has something in which they can take pride. But apparently you walk into Britain's factories and the first thing they do is strip this from you, to make you uniform, to make you malleable. But the reverse is true, you don't become malleable . . . in the end you become a little rebel. I think it is necessary to have a fellow who cares and who is trained then to learn to know men, and to set as his task, his responsibility, to ensure these people are getting fulfillment out of their job. And I believe that even in the most mundane job it can be done. If we're clever enough to do it.

I believe that the answer lies in training, the training of foremen, the training of managers, to realise the little things, and I'm not talking about . . . you know . . . building a vast new factory or anything like this because I don't believe any of it will work. I don't believe that if you poured more and more into their wage packets that you would change their attitudes. I believe that the repetitive process in factories is always going to produce the same situation until we change the way in which we manufacture, which I can't see coming for a very, very long time.

Well, I've looked at what makes men tick, or have tried to in my own small way. And I know there are a number of things: one, a man wants some sort of fulfillment out of his job and I have gone out — as I say, I have in all about 45 men — and I try to build a pride in those men in themselves. Not always been easy, you know, to search out their stronger points, where you're obviously not conning them, not giving them a load.

You know, if a man does a good job, a man's quality, then I complimented him on the quality of his work. If he's fast, and some fellows are, you know, I've observed and let him know that I'm aware of this and I appreciate it. Other blokes are neither fast or quality, but their time-keeping is immaculate; they are always there, always willing. Well, O.K., I find that the willingness is the quality that I'm looking for in that man.

Get them believing in themselves again instead of being just little cogs in a little machine that don't really matter. Well, this is one of the first things I try to do, you know, to give these blokes an awareness and a pride in themselves. And quite frankly, I honestly and sincerely believe, though this might sound arrogant from a foreman of six months, but I honestly and sincerely believe that I've brought these fellows along . . . I've let them grow at least six inches since I've been on the job.

Secondly, as I've said, we've three tracks side by side, you know. People will stand to watch a football match in far worse conditions than we've got in a factory, you know. They'll stand while it's belting down with rain and cramp and there it is . . . the competitiveness is so great you know. I try to instil a little of the competitive spirit into them. You know, we work against these tracks . . . or work against last week's figures.

I like stand on the end of the line at the end of the day and we've either achieved the programme before anyone else, or alternatively, if we've failed to achieve the programme through reasons beyond our control, we've got two or three bodies in there. I stand there . . . 'We are the champions' and they all think they're bloody idiots . . . but O.K., now they've taken it up. And they're proud of the fact that they're producing more than the other tracks. And I go around openly boasting about my whizz kids, my little angels on track nine, you know, where they can hear me and approach the job in this manner. And it works. Now as I say, I've only been on the job six months and I haven't access to records too far back, but I can say that my absenteeism is lower than anyone else, my production is greater and I seem to get a hell of a lot more co-operation. And I believe it is because, O.K., perhaps it's novel to them. I have to continually think ahead of them — to try and put a little something into their day.

It makes such a vast difference to see these blokes go out with a spring in their step and a smile on their face, and come in the same way, instead of walking in and out of the factory, you know, as if they hated every stick and stone in it. And I believe we've got to do this because I don't believe it's any man's right to subject men to the sort of purgatory you find in factories today. Purely and simply because no one has cared enough even in the smallest way to make them feel that they're wanted, that they're important, to give them a pride. You know you've got to instil this — it isn't something like we talk about craftsmen's pride, craft is finished in mass produced factories. There is no job fulfillment — unless we set new levels and new standards. You see, if they're thanked for what they're doing enough times, ultimately, they'll begin to think it's important and they will take a pride in achieving that. But I believe, you know, that people are environmental experts, or psychologists, sociology whizz kids.

If these could get down and put into our hands the means of trying to change the working life shape for these men, my God, we've really achieved something.

The company, the managers, have to change their values, because ultimately this is going to reflect, I believe, in quality and quantity, which is what we're all basically here for. I do not believe it is necessary to create robots and cabbages to produce it . . . and I think this has been demonstrated in industry today.

I think this rash of strikes and irrational behaviour, and that everything must be met in conflict and confrontation, is a result of this grass-root problem, of the alienation of the individual to his job, to his supervision, to his company. And I believe it is because the relationships, the human relationships, are wrong and I believe, equally sincerely, if we cry hard enough, the 'you's and 'I's of this world, someone will ultimately listen.

And that's what I've tried to convince myself, obviously for my own ego, on my little track in my huge factory — that it is possible. And it is not ego when I say that I am in the process of demonstrating that, in my own small way. But I mean, if I could convince you of how important this is to millions of people, *millions of people*, that if we could change this attitude, change the life style of their working day, and from this, you know, their wives, and their kids will be happier as well, instead of being kicked around the place . . . because you can't make the transformation from cabbage to human in minutes. You know, it takes a little time . . . .

Source: From a transcript of a tape recording produced by Rank Audio Industrial Services.

British strikes: how they look from the factory floor

J. J. Maling

We ought to keep a sense of proportion about Britain's strike record. For one thing, even if we were to treble the official figures for strikes, far more working days are lost through the common cold or accidents at work, and ten times more through unemployment.

Perhaps even more misunderstood is the way strikes occur. Most people seem to have an impression of an immensely powerful union organisation or irresponsible shop stewards calling out thousands of reluctant workers. Things often look a little different when you're at the sharp end, on the factory floor.

Not only are strikes not very frequent in most workplaces, but those which do occur are usually quite spontaneous and, more often than not, quite unorganised. Frequently the shop steward, and almost invariably the union's district office, only hears about them after they have started.

I'm told that some innocent television viewers believed that trade unionism as portrayed in *The Rag Trade* bore some resemblance to the real thing. (Incidentally, may I protest about those headlines like 'Ten thousand idle'. During the only prolonged official strike in which I was ever involved, I've never worked so hard in my life).

At the place where I worked the process of starting a strike was quite complicated. Some of us, the so-called manual workers, were hourly paid and the rest were weekly paid, working under 'staff' conditions. This second group did work which was just as manual as that done by the manual workers; it was purely arbitrary which section a worker fell into.

The management gleefully used this completely artificial arrangement on the principle of 'divide and rule'.

Strangely, quite a lot of the workers approved of this attitude. Staff members were inclined to be a bit toffee-nosed in their attitude towards the manual workers, as if they were one step up the ladder to the dizzy heights of management; and the manual workers sneered at the staff as bootlickers (or words to that effect) enjoying special privileges.

The truth was that there was little advantage in belonging to one group or the other. The higher pay of the manuals was just about balanced by the better pensions and more generous sick pay of the staff. On the rare occasions when the two sections were on strike together, nothing could have been less sympathetic than the sympathetic action of whichever group stood to gain nothing from the dispute.

Most strikes started with the manuals. There was a good reason for this; nothing to do with foreign agitators or reds under the bed. The manuals were very dependent on production bonuses which seldom seemed to have much connection with the amount of work they did, or with the actual production figures.

Of course not, for they were calculated in cosy offices by clerical workers far from the firing line. They weren't basing their conclusions on *production*, but on sheets of figures handed to them (and probably invented) by some middle management go-between. These bonuses were a constant and fruitful source of argument.

However, staff pay remained constant from week to week between pay reviews and all too often after them as well.

When a dispute arose the manual stewards would call a meeting. The staff workers would never be told about this, even if they were members of the same union, which most of them were. However, sometimes they found out inadvertently, and asked, with some justification, what was going on. Usually they were told to mind their own business, for in some circles they were regarded as spies for the management. (Undoubtedly some of them were, for the management was always well informed).

If the manual workers voted for a strike, the staff members, hearing of it by some means, would approach a shop steward and ask if they were expected to support the stoppage. Typically the day shift steward would say 'No, it's nothing to do with you,' and the night man 'Certainly.'

So the night staff would find themselves on strike while the day men worked on and there would be furious phoning in all directions for further information and instructions, in an effort to sort out the muddle. And just in case anyone thought of approaching the Union's Area Office for the official line, it wasn't worth the trouble, because mostly no one had even told them there *was* a dispute They would always be the last to know, and most strikes were sorted out locally by the stewards before they were told.

In these intriguing circumstances we would find particularly keen section managers going round the homes of the night staff telling them they were supposed to be working; while exceptionally astute stewards might well phone round first to tell their members not to answer the door.

If you get the impression that our union affairs were more than a little confused that would not be an unfair judgement.

But the attitude of the workers — both sorts — was crystal-clear, compared with that of the management, who had even less idea of what was going on than we did.

For them the usual sequence of events would be to issue the following orders to the supervisors in rapid and contrary succession:

(1) Stay at home, but you won't get paid.
(2) Stay at home and you will get paid.
(3) Come to work and work normally.
(4) Come to work, but don't do any.

Mind you, I'm only giving a rough idea of the thing; in practice there would be far more contradictory orders than that.

But, surprisingly, there is one good thing to be said for this seemingly crazy system. It works. Disagreements which have dragged on for months, causing bad feeling, bitterness, loss of production, and poor quality work, are rapidly resolved in nine cases out of ten as soon as there's the first whisper of a possible strike. (The tenth one is the one you read about in the papers).

Why? Well, because the workers don't want to lose too much money and the management don't want to lose too much production.

Source: Financial Times, 3 January 1979.

Some common terms and phrases — industrial relations

Absenteeism   Persistent or regular absence from work of an individual or group without a valid reason.

Advisory, conciliation and arbitration service (ACAS)
A body which gives advice and conciliation and provides for arbitration for employers and employee organis-ations. ACAS has specific responsibilities under the Employment Protection Act 1975 in disputes over such matters as trade union recognition by companies, disclosure of information to employees and time off for trade union activities. ACAS is financed by public money but is not controlled by the government.

Closed shop   Agreement between union and employer whereby employees must be trade union members. This can be a *pre-entry* closed shop in which a person must be a member of a union before he can be offered a job or *post-entry* in which the employee has to join the union on, or soon after, taking up employment.

Collective bargaining   The process by which the various terms and conditions of employment are settled by direct negotiation between representatives of employees and those of an employer or employer's association.

Conciliation   The bringing together of two parties involved in a dispute so that an outside party can establish any common ground and thus encourage them to reach a compromise.

Convener   The chief shop steward in a factory or department who brings together the committee of shop stewards at the works and is often secretary to this committee. He is generally brought in to help solve any problem that involves a large section of the workforce.

Demarcation   The agreed division of types of work or tasks between workers of different trades. Demarcation disputes may arise when the introduction of new equip-ment calls on employees to take on new tasks which may previously have been done by other groups.

Differentials   The difference between wage rates of workers with different degrees of skill employed in the same occupation or industry. These are preserved when increases are calculated on a percentage basis but eroded when flat rate increases are given, as at the time of the 1974 pay 'freeze'.

Discipline procedure   Rules laid down within a factory or industry by which management maintains discipline while ensuring that a fair procedure is consistently followed.

Grievance procedure   The rules laid down within a factory or industry by which problems and grievances of individuals should be settled.

Job evaluation   The process of determining objectively the level of one job in relation to another on which a fair pay structure can be based.

Last in, first out   A formula by which it is understood that if redundancy becomes necessary, the workers with the shortest service with the firm will be laid off first.

Lock out   A situation where the employer shuts the workers out of the works — the equivalent to a strike in reverse — which is seldom used.

Picketing   A demonstration by striking workers in front of the works to draw attention to their case and dissuade other workers from entering the firm and thereby weakening the effect of the strike.

Piecework   Payment is made on the basis of the volume of work done.

Plant bargaining   Negotiation between individual employers and their workers carried out at factory, as opposed to national, level.

Strike   The action by which workers withdraw their labour, that is refuse to work, as a means of putting pressure on their employer. These are *official* if approved by the union and *unofficial* if not. Sudden unofficial strikes may be called *wild-cat* strikes.

Discussion

The following questions could be used as a basis for a general discussion, or possibly a debate, on various aspects of industrial relations. Alternatively the highly complex relationship between management and employees could be looked at using the case studies and role play that conclude this chapter.

(1) It is sometimes said that the interests of managers and workers inevitably conflict. Is this true?
(2) Do you think there is a strong feeling of 'them and us' in British industry? Can you cite any evidence to support your view?
(3) What positive steps can be taken to increase co-operation between management and employees?
(4) Would you go on strike? Does your attitude to striking vary with the different types of jobs people do?
(5) Two controversial aspects of trade unionism are
   • The closed shop, and
   • Picketing.

Do you think these should be allowed? If so, should there be any legislation to control their use?

(6) Collect as much information as you can find on a well-publicised strike that has taken place recently. Trace the events leading up to the strike, the strike's effect on the company and the employees involved and its resolution. Where did things go wrong? Could the problems have been avoided?

(7) Supposing there were no trade unions as we know them in Britain. Can you imagine how the present union role might be carried out? Would it be necessary to develop other representative bodies? Could each employee interact with his employer as an individual? How, for example, could agreement be reached on pay?

(8) What factors have influenced the development of industrial relations as we see it today? Are these factors still operating?

Class activity

The shop steward's responsibilities — case study

It is important to remember that when people are elected by their fellow workers to act as employee representatives — whether they serve on, for example, a staff committee or as shop stewards — their prime responsibility is to those whom they represent. The supervisor, on the other hand, is management's representative and is accountable to management. Sometimes these roles become confused, as happened in this case.

The problem

Tony Fraser had been a shop steward in his department for 10 years. He got on very well with the department manager, *Bob Hardy*, who was surprised when Tony came to his office one day to introduce the new steward, *Brian Stone*. Brian had just been elected, and Tony was as puzzled as Hardy as to why he had not been re-elected after representing the workers for all those years.

After the introduction, Brian Stone requested a meeting with Hardy as soon as possible to raise certain issues. When they had gone, Bob Hardy talked the matter over with *Jack Wild*, one of his foremen. Jack was not surprised at the change. He seemed to have seen it coming for some time.

Hardy was annoyed, saying that even his 'choice of friends' was being dictated by the union. 'I didn't influence Tony,' he said.

'Because I respect and like the man I was able to confide in him. Tony is a reliable sort, which is more than I can say for Stone, a militant troublemaker if ever I saw one.

'Of course I used Tony, and to the men's advantage if only they could see it. How else would they get to know my decisions concerning them? I always listened to the points that Tony raised, and when they clamoured for more money I explained our financial position carefully to him. He could see and understand that you can't wring blood from a stone. And I left the disciplining of troublemakers to him rather than dealing with it myself. The fools don't know when they are well off.'

'Perhaps that's half the problem,' muttered Jack under his breath. 'Even the foremen don't get the access to information that Tony has had.' He told Hardy

'Stone should make a good steward. He has done evening classes in industrial relations, which is more than Tony ever has, and when we were stuck over the introduction of work study Stone was the one who worked it out for the men. Also Tony hasn't attended a union branch meeting for months.'

'Well I suppose we shall have to put up with Stone,' replied Hardy. 'But I sometimes wish I was a union member myself. That might change a few things.'

Taking his new deputy steward with him, Brian Stone went to see Hardy on the following morning with a list of points to discuss. The most important of these were that

- He was not prepared to act as a management messenger boy.
- The employees were unhappy that the grievance procedure was not being used properly by management and problems were taking an unreasonable length of time to resolve, apparently because the foremen had to refer all of them to Hardy before giving their men an answer.
- The employees were fed up with never being consulted over changes before they were introduced.
- He wanted to establish a system of regular meetings with his members in company time to discuss departmental matters, as well as regular meetings between management and the shop stewards.

Hardy was completely taken aback by these requests and could only reply that he needed time to think them over. 'Tony was always in the picture about what was going on and he didn't keep asking for meetings,' he thought to himself. This session had lasted two hours and now he would have to spend more time coming up with some answers. Everything had been far easier before . . . .

Discussion

(1) Was Bob Hardy right in lamenting the end of the old way of things?
(2) Was it in fact to his and management's advantage to have the shop steward on their side?
(3) Was Bob Hardy's attitude towards the union a sensible one?
(4) Where did Tony Fraser go wrong?
(5) Was Brian Stone really a 'militant troublemaker'?
(6) Do you think his requests were unreasonable?

A question of discipline — case study

In industrial relations, as with so many aspects of working in industry, one of the most crucial areas is that where a supervisor or manager and those he supervises meet. The vast majority of industrial relations problems are settled at this level, perhaps with the involvement of the shop steward or staff representative, rather than through discussions between senior management and trade union officials.

This is particularly so with problems involving discipline or grievances, where the agreed procedures usually start at the level of the employee and supervisor concerned, unless a large group of people are involved. It is a sound industrial relations principle that problems should be resolved at the lowest possible level.

Take this example which took place in the machine shop of an engineering works.

The problem

William McNab has been foreman of the machine shop for over 10 years and has managed to keep a good team of men. One of these is *Ted Merritt*, who has been in the department for three years and is one of the best operators. McNab and Ted are friendly and often meet in the club for a drink and a game of billiards.

When it was suggested two months ago that because the department had expanded McNab needed an assistant foreman, he recommended Ted who was promoted. He seemed to settle in well, although he still had a lot to learn, and McNab was satisfied.

The factory canteen would get very crowded at lunch-time, and if you were too far back in the queue, you often had only the less popular food to choose from. To avoid this some employees had got into the habit of leaving their departments a few minutes early. On this occasion Ted Merritt had seen *Harry Bishop*, a machine shop operator, going into the canteen five minutes before lunch-time. He called Bishop back and asked him where he was off to. 'To the canteen, of course,' said Bishop.

Ted ordered him back to work but Bishop became angry and abusive, calling him a spy. By this time the whistle had gone. Ted tried to calm Bishop down but his temper got worse so Ted warned him that he would be reported.

Ted went to see McNab as soon as he could on the following day. Soon after this Bishop came to see McNab and apologised, asking him to ignore the incident because of his good record. He had been with the company a good deal longer than Ted.

Discussion

If you were the foreman what would you do, both to solve the immediate problem and to prevent the same thing happening again? Remember that if handled badly this sort of situation can lead to far more serious and widespread industrial relations problems. In your answer you might consider the following questions:

(1) Was Ted Merritt justified in ordering Bishop back to work?
(2) When Bishop lost his temper, could the situation have been handled differently?
(3) What action, if any, should McNab have taken when the matter was reported to him?
(4) If McNab accepts Bishop's apology, will he undermine Ted's authority in the machine shop?
(5) If McNab supports Ted, what penalty could he impose?
(6) Should the problem of time-keeping at lunch-time be tackled in the machine shop only?
(7) Is it inevitable that the first in the canteen queue get the best choice of food?

(8) Is the canteen service adequate?

(9) Does the problem reveal a weakness in the method used to promote Ted Merritt?

The build-up — case study

Often in industry a series of minor misunderstandings can lead to a confrontation between management and employees which may result in strike action. Sometimes this could have been avoided. Take this case which took place on a building site.

The problem

One morning the architect and the site agent, *Mr Blake,* were inspecting the site when the architect remarked that the finish of the concrete on the main staircase might be considered unsatisfactory. When they reached the staircase the carpenter, *Ken,* who was working on it, overheard the architect say, 'It's no good. It'll have to be done again.'

After the architect had left, Blake, already late for a meeting, told site foreman, *Harry Barkham,* to take Ken off the job because of a change of plan. He gave no details. Harry spoke to Ken who, thinking his work was being criticised, would not leave the job. As a result, Harry sacked Ken for refusing to obey an order.

As Ken was on his way to collect his cards he met one of his mates and they went to the canteen to talk over the incident. Here Ken explained to his shop steward, *Terry Fisher,* what had happened and claimed he was being victimised. Terry went to phone the union organiser from a call box, but he could not get through. Ken's mates then decided to take matters into their own hands and refused, in spite of Terry's attempts to persuade them to the contrary, to go back to work until Ken had got satisfaction.

When Harry, the foreman, heard of the decision he threatened to sack the lot of them. Terry suggested that he and Harry discuss the situation in the office. They agreed that it was difficult, particularly because they were both fairly new to the job and Harry had had trouble with Ken before. They tried to contact the site agent, but the agent had left no details of his movements with his secretary.

Terry then agreed to talk to the men once more, but before he could do so was called to a meeting of all site shop stewards by the site convener, *Ron Price,* who had heard of the problem. At this discussion other minor unsettled grievances were raised and the stewards decided to hold a meeting of all the men at 1600 hours. At this meeting they agreed on their conditions for resumption of work.

Meanwhile Blake had returned to the site and demanded to know why work was at a standstill. Harry explained what had happened and Blake sent for Ron Price who told him the men's conditions for going back to work, one of which was Ken's reinstatement. The site agent refused to discuss this while the men were out and then rang head office for advice.

Discussion

In the space of a few hours an apparently smoothly operating construction site has been brought to a standstill by a situation which has built up with alarming ease.

(1) What went wrong and how could the problem have been avoided?

(2) What action should the site agent now take to remedy the situation?

Shop steward's negotiations — role play

This role play is intended to give an idea of what a negotiation between management and employee representatives may be like. As is often the case, the subject under dispute is not really a major one, but each side nevertheless has its own view of the matter.

Six students are recommended to act out the role play while the others watch and observe the different

It's no good, it'll have to be done again...

attitudes and behaviour patterns that the negotiators exhibit. Before meeting across the table the three trade union and management representatives should meet in separate groups for not more than 15 minutes to prepare their strategy for the negotiations. They should list the points they are going to make and decide who should speak on each. One of the observers should keep a record of the proceedings which can be used when analysing the discussion. The meeting should not last for more than 20 minutes and should be chaired by the general manager.

The case concerns a toy-making factory at which management has notified its intention of taking away the afternoon tea break. Details are given below.

The agreement of the tea break

Following representations from the shop stewards the tea break was first granted by management two years ago on the following conditions:

(1) The tea was to be brought to the workers on trolleys: they were not to go to the canteen where they took their morning break.
(2) The break was to last 10 minutes and was to be regarded as a concession.
(3) Any misuse of the concession would mean that it would be withdrawn.

The withdrawal of the tea break

The concession has been abused consistently during the last six months in Department *A* where employees were repeatedly off the job for more than 10 minutes. This could not be explained by breakdowns in the trolley service. It has not happened in Department *B*.

The foreman of Department *A* spoke to the steward and warned him that if this problem continued, he would have to recommend to the manager that the tea break be withdrawn. During these six months three warnings had been given in accordance with company procedure. The steward did not convey these warnings to the convening steward.

After the third warning the foreman reported to the manager who put up the following notice without consulting the convening steward:

'Despite warnings, the concession of a 10-minute tea break in the afternoon has continued to be abused. As from Monday this concession will therefore be withdrawn.'

Factory details

The total number of employees is 200, of whom 180 are trade union members. Department *A* has 60 women and 40 men, and Department *B*, 90 women and 10 men. The hours of work on a five-day week are

Monday–Thursday:	0800–1300 and 1400–1800
Friday:	0800–1300 and 1400–1700

Department *B* is the department where the toys are assembled and packed. In Department *A* the plastic is prepared and moulded. Department *A* is hot and dusty compared with Department *B*.

The toilet facilities in the factory are adequate.

The factory is covered by the Toy Trade Wages Council, although the wages paid are slightly higher than the rate set by the Council.

Negotiating procedure

The factory was first organised by the union during the war. Management recognises and negotiates with the union, although they are more willing to meet the stewards than officials of the union.

There are three stewards recognised — one each in Department *A* and *B* and a convening steward who works in Department *B*.

The recognised negotiating procedure is for the departmental stewards to take up individual or departmental complaints with their foreman. Failing settlement, the convening steward sees the manager. Where a dispute affects all employees the convening steward, together with his departmental stewards, usually meets the manager, who is accompanied by his personnel officer and the foreman.

Management

The manager, whose attitude is 'fatherly', is the grandson of the founder of the firm which is a family business. Each of the two departments has a foreman and there is a personnel officer who is also the chief wages clerk.

Negotiation

The following take part in the negotiation:

Representing the employees:

The *convening steward* — an experienced steward who has worked with the company in Department *B* for 15 years. He has been a trade union member for 20 years.

The *Department A steward* — a younger, less experienced steward with a temper and a strong dislike for his foreman.

The *Department B steward* — a recently appointed steward with little experience in negotiation, but who has handled his job well to date.

Representing the employers:

The *general manager* — a middle-aged man with a somewhat mild manner, who adopts a benevolent but autocratic attitude towards his employees.

The *foreman of Department A* — appointed two years ago, after four years as a chargehand, and two as a moulder. He was never a member of the union, and does not believe in them.

The *personnel officer/wages clerk* — appointed two years ago. He is not a man of definite views and usually reflects, while attempting to appear neutral, the views of the general manager.

Industry in Society

13

A good deal has been said and written about the social irresponsibility of industry, its effect on the environment, its drive to make profits at the expense of those it employs, and so on. It is important, therefore, when looking at the place of industry in society to establish exactly to whom it is responsible and to what degree.

There are five main sectors which make demands on companies and to which they are directly or indirectly responsible.

- The *shareholders* — who provide the finance necessary to run the company which in turn has a legal obligation to look after their investment.
- Its *employees* — without them the company could not function and in return for their work the company pays them a wage.
- Its *customers* — if they are not satisfied, they will buy elsewhere.
- The *local community* — from here the company draws the bulk of its workforce and its image amongst local people is important.
- The *country* — the company is bound by the laws of the country and must be influenced by national policy. Its success or failure, together with that of the rest of British industry, is closely tied up with the future of the country as a whole and its position in world trade.

From this list you can see that industry has not only a moral obligation to those involved with it, but it is also essential to its own success to see that their demands are satisfied. This has been aptly called: 'following a policy of enlightened self-interest'.

So far so good, but many of the difficulties encountered by industry's decision-makers are a result of the fact that you can *please* some of the people all the time, and all the people some of the time, but you can't *please* all the people all the time (with apologies to Abraham Lincoln).

Inevitably the claims of some of the groups we have mentioned conflict with those of others. For example, to install extremely expensive pollution controlling

equipment will delight the local community and probably the country as a whole, but it may mean a lower return for the shareholders, less money to finance wage increases for employees, and might necessitate price rises which would not please the customers.

Equally a holiday airline may please its customers by operating regular early morning flights at reduced rates, but the people living near the airport are likely to protest and the employees may not appreciate working these 'unsocial' hours.

Management is, therefore, often faced with the need to compromise. Bearing in mind those who will be affected by its decision, it has to try to agree on a course of action that will give maximum benefit and cause minimum harm.

Included here are two articles to illustrate some of the arguments on the social responsibility of industry. The first by John Humble, a management consultant and affiliate professor of INSEAD (the European Institute of Business Administration) was published in 1976. The second was written by John Ruskin in the first half of the nineteenth century and shows that a lot of what we are saying today is not new, but has been so since man first started producing goods and services and exchanging them for money.

Social responsibility: the heart of business

John Humble

Endless debate about whether business has or has not social responsibility is misconceived. It is at the heart of every business, not an 'optional extra'. The development of a healthy community requires the contribution of many institutions, each of which is unique. The Church has a spiritual purpose; universities and schools are focal points of learning. Business has the more prosaic task of creating economic wealth, without which phrases like quality of life become hypocrisy. When business performance declines, this truth becomes a painful reality. Bankrupt companies do not provide jobs and economically weak countries cannot sustain generous social security systems.

Since society is in an unprecedented state of turbulent change — technological, social, political and economic — it is hardly surprising that *every* institution is being criticised. Business is no exception. As the American sociologist Daniel Bell puts it, in the post-industrial world 'the sense of identity between self-interest of the corporation and the public has been replaced by a sense of incongruence'. What then should business do?

A company must have explicit policies of the same quality and depth for social and public affairs as for marketing, production and finance. This is already happening. In 1970, 38 per cent of a sample of 100 U.S. companies in the 'Top 500' had social goals in their planning process; by 1973 it was 64 per cent and by now it will be even higher. Policies can only be developed after asking some searching questions. Do we only obey the strict letter of the law or do we go beyond it in selected areas? Shall we lag or lead in relation to the rest of our industry? Should we participate in creating codes of conduct, such as the OECD code for multinational enterprises, and, if so, how do we ensure the codes are followed in practice? An increasing number of companies are now analysing

systematically their social impact through special audits or task force studies. Health and safety, equal opportunity, product safety, fair advertising, ecologically sound packaging are all areas requiring careful study. Unless business willingly takes initiatives it must accept the ever increasing volume of social legislation without complaint.

Developing corporate strategies which anticipate and respond constructively to social demands presents practical difficulties. First, measurement tools are unsophisticated in many important social areas. To rely too much on quantified data alone can lead to an Oscar Wilde position where we 'know the price of everything but the value of nothing'. Given limited resources and inadequate measurements how can a company confidently trade off less pollution against more education and training? Second, whose values are the decisions to be based on? Ralph Nader and others feel strongly that social audits must be made by outside objective social auditors, not by the company itself. But on many issues there is no real objectivity, merely opinions. In my view, managers possess corporate concern, integrity and self-criticism to levels comparable with other members of society; they can be trusted to make their own studies in co-operation with qualified experts in special fields like pollution.

Need for corporate policies

The multinational enterprise faces an even more complex problem in values. Should it take the view that in each country where it works it should be a good citizen, in the fullest sense, by the values of that community? Or should there be values common to the whole corporation? Third, public disclosure of the information on social performance is a powerful motivator to change. Progressive companies welcome this and often give leadership in disclosing more

than is legally required. One difficulty is that if the disclosure is not reasonably universal it may place a company at trading disadvantage with its sometimes less responsible international competitors. Fourth, the classic decentralised profit centre organisation* pattern does not readily facilitate effective social response. Traditional planning and financial control systems are less than adequate at explaining and evaluating significant areas of social concern. Moreover the rewards system for division managers often concentrates on short-term operational matters rather than complex longer-term social impacts.

The need for corporate policies and leadership is clear. Equally clear is the fact that social policies can only be effective when they are built naturally into the regular management system of the enterprise. Experiments in new structure; more systematic environmental scanning; supplementary information systems; sensitive use of special advisers — these are some of the 'nuts and bolts' a company has to work on if it is to convert worthy policies into action.

Constructive dialogue

A great deal of tension arises from sheer misunderstanding. Surveys indicate that public confidence in business integrity is deteriorating. Words like 'profits' usually conjure up responses such as 'greed' and 'exploitation' simply because the simple economic facts of life are not well communicated. For example, ICI in 1975 made a survey in Britain on views of profits. At first sight the results were encouraging since 83 per cent of those interviewed endorsed the belief that profitability safeguarded jobs. However, only 44 per cent thought the results were presented honestly — 'manipulation

* Where individual units of a firm have to account for profitability in their own right

of figures', 'agreements between dishonest accountants and companies' and 'evasion of law' were viewed as the three most likely offences.

Increasingly, business is presenting to its own employees and to the community at large an honest appraisal of its basic social contribution. This is not a cosmetic job of masking the ugly face of capitalism. A Norwegian insurance company, in a social report accompanying the annual accounts, analyses its co-operation with health research organisations and its campaigns to counter drug abuse. The report starts, however, with a fundamental statement on the social role of insurance in Norwegian society — that is at the heart of its business. Communications are also more generally perceived as constructive dialogue, not just telling the company's story. General Motors has a Board sub-committee of non-executive directors which enquires into all phases of the corporation's business activities that relate to matters of public policy. Critics, radical groups, politicians — anyone wishing to express a view and join in discussion is welcomed. Another company — Eaton — encourages all its managers to get out into the community and start a dialogue with student and citizen groups on what their business is doing, the place of free enterprise and so on.

A matter of priorities

One reason why business disappoints the community is that the expectations placed on it are unreasonably high. In spite of a barrage of criticisms business is still perceived as the institution which gets things done. Clearly, it becomes counter-productive when business is asked to solve complex problems which are the responsibility of democratically elected governments. Business can work in partnership with government on problems such as urban development, equitable distribution of wealth within a country and between rich and poor nations; the prohibition of certain drugs; social justice for minority groups and so on. But business alone has not the authority to deal with these problems alone and must firmly refuse responsibility for them.

Of course, business can and must accept full responsibility for minimising or removing undesirable impacts caused by its own existence and activities. For example, responsibility for safe products, good working conditions, reduced pollution of air, water and land. With limited resources, action must concentrate on a few priorities. A sample of 68 companies in the EEC gave their priorities overall as:

(1) Responding to demands of organised labour.
(2) Providing wide opportunities for employees to participate in decisions which affect them.
(3) Complying with new social legislation.

Every company ought to have its own priority list worked out. Even where an analysis is objective and perceptive the fair course of action in terms of social justice is complex. A study of 63 major integrated steel mills in the United States to assess the economic impact of just one Environmental Protection Agency rule (i.e. water pollution must be managed to the level of the best practicable technology) revealed that 11 old mills might have to close, displacing 33 000 workers. What then is social responsibility? A clean town but no jobs? A longer time scale to reach the standard? The more forceful critics of business so often have neat, simple and speedy solutions for problems which in truth are bewilderingly complex.

Business, like all other major institutions, must respond constructively to the changing expectations and evolving values of society at large. It will be judged by two interlocking criteria. First, it is expected to make the most effective use of human, physical and financial resources to produce goods, services and foundations of economic wealth for the community. Second, economic performance must be matched by a profound concern for the human consequences and social justice of every business decision. Whether it is developing a new product, selecting an investment area, closing down an obsolete plant, the wishes of all stakeholders must be taken into consideration.

There is ample evidence that business has the leadership, sense of corporate citizenship, management capability and will to meet this great challenge.

Source: Unilever Magazine, November/December 1976

Unto this last

John Ruskin

The fact is, that people never have had clearly explained to them the true functions of a merchant with respect to other people. I should like the reader to be very clear about this.

Five great intellectual professions, relating to daily necessities of life, have hitherto existed — three exist necessarily, in every civilised nation:

- The soldier's profession is to defend it
- The pastor's, to teach it
- The physician's, to keep it in health
- The lawyer's, to enforce justice in it
- The merchant's, to provide for it.

And the duty of all these men is, on due occasion, to die for it.

On due occasion, namely:

- The soldier, rather than leave his post in battle
- The physician, rather than leave his post in plague
- The pastor, rather than teach falsehood
- The lawyer, rather than countenance injustice
- The merchant — what is his 'due occasion' of death?

It is the main question for the merchant, as for all of us. For, truly, the man who does not know when to die, does not know how to live.

Observe the merchant's function (or manufacturer's, for in the broad sense in which it is here used the word must be understood to include both) is to provide for the nation. It is no more his function to get profit for himself out of that provision than it is a clergyman's function to get his stipend. The stipend is a due and necessary adjunct, but not the object, of his life, if he be a true clergyman, any more than his fee (or honorarium) is the object of life to a true physician.

Neither is his fee the object of life to a true merchant. All three, if true men, have a work to be done irrespective of fee — to be done even at any cost, or for quite the contrary of fee; the pastor's function being to teach, the physician's to heal, and the merchant's, as I have said, to provide.

And because the production or obtaining of any commodity involves necessarily the agency of many lives and hands, the merchant becomes in the course of his business the master and governor of large masses of men in a more direct, though less confessed way, than a military officer or pastor; so that on him falls, in great part, the responsibility for the kind of life they lead: and it becomes his duty, not only to be always considering how to produce what he sells in the purest and cheapest forms, but how to make the various employments involved in the production, or transference of it, most beneficial to the men employed.

And as into these two functions, requiring for their right exercise the highest intelligence, kindness, and tact, the merchant is bound to put all his energy, so for their just discharge he is bound, as soldier or physician is bound, to give up, if need be, his life, in such a way as it may be demanded of him. Two main points he has in his providing function to maintain: first, his engagements (faithfulness to engagements being the real root of all possibilities in commerce); and, secondly, the perfectness and purity of the thing provided — so that, rather than fail any engagement, or consent to any deterioration, adulteration, or unjust and exhorbitant price of that which he provides, he is bound to meet fearlessly any form of distress, poverty, or labour, which may, through maintenance of these points, come upon him.

Again: in his office as governor of the men employed by him, the merchant or manufacturer is invested with a distinctly paternal authority and responsibility. In most cases a youth entering a commercial establishment is withdrawn altogether from home influence; his master must become his father, else he has, for practical and constant help, no father at hand: in all cases the master's authority, together with the general tone and atmosphere of his business and the character of the men with whom the youth is compelled in the course of it to associate, have more immediate and pressing weight than the home influence, and will usually neutralise it either for good or evil — so that the only means the master has of doing justice to the men employed by him is to ask himself sternly whether he is dealing with such subordinate as he would with his own son, if compelled by circumstances to take such a position.

Supposing the captain of a frigate saw it right, or were by chance obliged, to place his own son in the position of a common sailor; as he would then treat his son, he is bound always to treat every one of the men under him. So, also, supposing the master of a manufactory saw it right, or were by any chance obliged, to place his own son in the position of an ordinary workman; as he would then treat his son, he is bound always to treat every one of his men. This is the only effective, true or practical rule which can be given on this point of political economy.

And as the captain of a ship is bound to be the last man to leave his ship in case of wreck, and to share his last crust with the sailors in case of famine, so the manufacturer, in any commercial crisis or distress, is bound to take the suffering of it with his men, and even to take more of it for himself than he allows his men to feel; as a father would in famine, shipwreck or battle, sacrifice himself for his son.

All of which sounds very strange: the only real strangeness in the matter being, nevertheless, that it should so sound. For all this is true, and that not partially nor theoretically, but everlastingly and practically: all other doctrine than this respecting matters political being false in premises, absurd in deduction, and impossible in practice, consistently with any progressive state of national life; all the life which we now possess as a nation showing itself in the resolute denial and scorn, by a few strong minds and faithful hearts, of economic principles taught to our multitudes, which principles, so far as accepted, lead straight to national destruction . . . .

Class activity

Exercise and discussion

The following exercise should help to establish the types of conflicting demands which industry sometimes has to face.

(1) Divide the class into five more or less equal groups. Each group represents one of the sectors to which a manufacturing company may be responsible, that is shareholders, employees, customers, the local community and the country. Each should draw up a list of the 10 most important steps it would wish the company to take to benefit that particular group. Rank these in order of priority. Each group should then choose a spokesman to make a brief presentation to 'management' explaining its choices and the justification for them.

(2) If you then analyse all five lists you may find that certain of the priorities of one group conflict with those of the others. Weigh them up against one another and prepare a 10-point plan for management.

(3) How could you justify each of these 10 points to the groups that would not benefit from them? For example, could you make a short presentation to shareholders at the annual general meeting

explaining your plan of action and the reason you
have included the various points?

(4) Does your compromise solution come down more
on the side of one group or another? If so, why?

The importance of profit

Closely linked with the idea of the role of industry
in society is that of whether it is morally right for
companies to make profits. However, whatever one's
priorities for industry are, it is an inescapable fact
that unless a company is profitable it is not, in the
long term, going to be able to fulfil its responsibilities
to any of the groups we have been considering.

But what is in fact meant by 'profitable'? Perhaps
the best way of looking at profit is through the concept
of added value.

The concept of added value

Manufacturers purchase the raw materials needed to
make a product which they then sell. The difference
between the selling price and the combined cost of
these raw materials, of company overheads such as
rent and of necessary outside services, such as electricity
and computer time, can be thought of as the value the
people working have added by the manufacturing
process. This 'added value' is used to pay wages to
employees, dividends to shareholders, taxes to the
government and for reinvestment.

If a company does not succeed in adding sufficient
value to cover all these things it will lose more and more
money, until eventually, if it is not bailed out by an
outside source, it will go bankrupt.

This will leave its employees with no jobs, its
shareholders with no investment, its customers with
no goods or services, and the community and country
with no taxes to help provide the schools, hospitals,
and other social services we enjoy.

The illustrations on pages 110 and 111 show the
way two companies explain added value to those who
work for them. The added value statements reproduced
here are taken from the Boots company report to staff
for 1977 and the Thorn Electrical 1978 special report
for employees. Thorn also gives an idea of what the
£55m the firm paid in taxes would pay for in terms of
community services.

The following article shows how one leading industrialist,
Sir Hector Laing, chairman of United Biscuits, sees the
added value equation in practice. Sir Hector argues that
added value is the key to economic prosperity.

The case for added value

Sir Hector Laing

The effect of North Sea oil on our
balance of payments provides us with a
short breathing space in which to correct
mistakes and plan a strategy for the
future which will enable us to restore
our competitive position in the world.
The balance of payments surplus which
the oil gives us may not continue for as
long as some optimists suggest, and a
strong currency which is not reinforced
by a strong industrial performance is not
conducive to long-term prosperity. Will
a nation work harder when things are
easier than when they were tough? I
doubt it. Unless attitudes are changed,
we will miss the opportunity which oil
offers.

There has prevailed for many decades,
if not centuries, a sort of intellectual
snobbery about trade and industry
being somehow inferior to the classical
branches of learning and to the professions. Kenneth Adams, of St George's
House, Windsor, put his finger on the
problem when he said 'There is a profound need for a change of attitude
within our society towards the activity
by which it earns its living. A society
which does not deeply believe in the
worthwhileness of the activity by
which it lives and, therefore, does not
hold that activity in reasonably high
esteem, faces a major moral dilemma
which will prevent it having a hopeful
and positive attitude towards its whole
future'; and we now appear to have a
prejudice against providing incentives
for effort and risk-taking and against
allowing a person to keep a fair share
of the rewards won for enterprise and
ingenuity. Somebody said that the
tragedy of the British working man is
the poverty of his ambition. The tragedy
of management in this country has been
the poverty of its vision. Management
must take up the challenge of leading
more dynamically and communicating
more effectively in order to win the
support and backing of employees for
wealth-creating policies. In a nation
where mistrust and ignorance have
been major factors in our post-war
decline and where historic class conflict
still aggravates industrial relations, that
support will not be obtained unless
people really understand the economic
realities. I believe that the best vehicle
management can use in explaining the
importance of investment and the
necessity for profitability is the concept
of added value — because it is simple
to explain and easy to understand and
it seems to me, the arithmetic cannot be
faulted.

What is added value?

The generally accepted definition is that
it is 'the difference between what a
company is paid for its products and
the cost of bought-in materials and
services'. Quite simply, it represents
the value of the conversion process.
The wealth so created has to pay for:

● *Employees* (the people who invest
their time in the company): wages,

salaries, national insurance, and employee benefits, including pensions

- *Capital* (the people who invest their savings in the company): interest and dividends
- *Reinvestment*: expenditure on new machinery, buildings, etc.
- *Taxation*: financing government expenditure

The creation of added value (the conversion process) requires the investment of

(a) *Capital*: in machinery, buildings, stocks, etc.
(b) *Employees*: to operate the machinery and to carry out distribution, selling, administrative operations.

But the most critical factors in establishing the amount of added value are substantially outside the company's control. These are

(1) The price the consumer is prepared to pay for the product.
(2) The cost of employees, i.e. the remuneration required to attract and hold the best possible calibre of employees at every level of the business.
(3) The cost of capital, the return required to attract and hold investors.

If the cost of employees or of capital is too high then the price of the product will be higher than the consumer is prepared to pay, sales will decline and ultimately the company will fail. Unless overall added value is increased in real terms, no one sector can get more except at the expense of another. Where other sectors gain at the expense of re-investment it is a recipe for disaster. Only by consistently ensuring that adequate funds are invested in machinery incorporating the latest technologies and research into new products will a company be able to provide:

- Employees with job security and an improving standard of living; a better working environment and an improving standard of living, and projects which create new jobs
- Shareholders with long-term security for their capital and improved real earnings per share
- Consumers with improved quality

and service, and better value for money through new technologies to improve efficiency.

Many employees believe they should receive a greater share of the wealth created — which they can:

- Unwisely, by insisting on being rewarded so highly that they price the products they are making out of the market and so price themselves out of a job
- Unwisely, by insisting on taking in wage increases some of the funds which should be allocated to re-investment for their future security — again putting jobs at risk
- Wisely, by working more efficiently and sharing the extra wealth created among the same number of people or even among fewer.

Many investors believe they can get a greater return on their investment — which they can:

- Unwisely, by demanding dividend increases at the expense of reinvestment
- Wisely, by recognising that in some years they may have to forgo dividend increases in order to provide for greater reinvestment which will generate increased wealth in the longer term.

Many consumers believe they can be insulated from increases in world commodity prices — which they cannot. Except in the very short term consumers cannot be protected by a system of price control which erodes added value and, therefore, limits reinvestment. Successful industrial countries have shown that prosperity depends upon the working population solidly backing the aims and objectives of its leaders in government and industry. Our nation will only succeed in competing effectively with other industrialised nations if it produces goods which the consumer at home and abroad considers good value for money. In so doing, it must offer a fair return to those who provide the capital as well as to those who provide their labour. To avoid being controlled by government-imposed prices and incomes policies which extend bureaucracy and stifle enterprise and initiative, we must learn self-discipline; only possible when there is understanding. I believe that the

following strategy to achieve understanding and banish mistrust would form a foundation on which to build, with enthusiasm and goodwill, a regenerated private industrial sector and greater wealth for the nation. Provided that the employees in a company agree to allocate to reinvestment a sufficient percentage of the added value to keep that company internationally competitive, and to match the added value per employee of that same competition, a company should in return:

- Guarantee to its employees a given percentage of the added value; this provides an opportunity for genuine participation
- Guarantee job security or income protection related to length of service
- Provide a salary structure designed to give reward for responsibility at all levels (it is the government's responsibility to ensure that this is not nullified by excessive taxation)
- Operate some form of assisted share purchase scheme so that as many employees as wished could become full shareholding members of their company
- Enable working members who are not shareholders to participate with shareholders at Annual General or Extraordinary Meetings.

A policy based on the above principles would provide the best possible chance of regenerating our industrial performance so that we would again be able to compete effectively with those trading nations whose commitment, whose level of added value per head, and whose more enlightened view on wealth-creation have enabled them to raise the standard of living of their peoples at a faster rate than we have.

Source: Industrial Society, July/ August 1978

Value Added

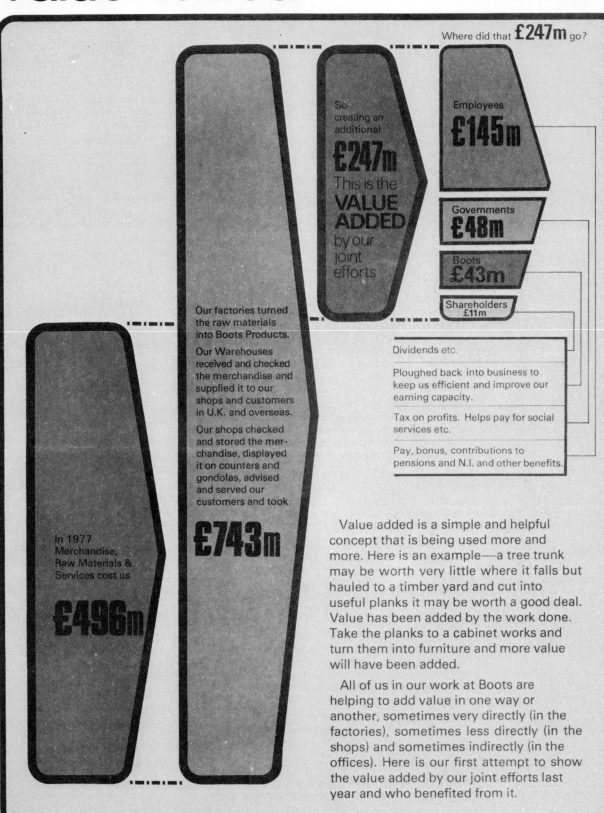

Where did that £247m go?

So creating an additional

£247m

This is the **VALUE ADDED** by our joint efforts

Employees **£145m**

Governments **£48m**

Boots **£43m**

Shareholders £11m

Dividends etc.

Ploughed back into business to keep us efficient and improve our earning capacity.

Tax on profits. Helps pay for social services etc.

Pay, bonus, contributions to pensions and N.I. and other benefits.

Our factories turned the raw materials into Boots Products.

Our Warehouses received and checked the merchandise and supplied it to our shops and customers in U.K. and overseas.

Our shops checked and stored the merchandise, displayed it on counters and gondolas, advised and served our customers and took

£743m

In 1977 Merchandise, Raw Materials & Services cost us

£496m

Value added is a simple and helpful concept that is being used more and more. Here is an example—a tree trunk may be worth very little where it falls but hauled to a timber yard and cut into useful planks it may be worth a good deal. Value has been added by the work done. Take the planks to a cabinet works and turn them into furniture and more value will have been added.

All of us in our work at Boots are helping to add value in one way or another, sometimes very directly (in the factories), sometimes less directly (in the shops) and sometimes indirectly (in the offices). Here is our first attempt to show the value added by our joint efforts last year and who benefited from it.

(a) Added value as Boots explained it to its employees

Source: Boots Company Report to Staff 1977

Added value

Total Income
£1,092m

Value Added to the
raw materials by
work done to them
£503m

Cost of raw
materials
and services
£589m

Pay and related costs **£304m**

Financing charges **£6m**

Replacement of plant
and equipment **£91m**

Tax to the
Government **£55m**

Dividends **£16m**

Profit for reinvestment **£31m**

You can be VATMAN and I'll be Robbing..

Added Value is the difference between the final selling price of a
product and the initial cost of the raw materials and services.

Everyone who works for Thorn is adding to the value
of these raw materials and services by participating in the
manufacturing process, by transporting and storing goods,
by recording their whereabouts and by selling them.

How the added value to the goods by our joint efforts is
distributed can be seen from the diagram. We as individuals and
Thorn the Company all benefit from added value.

(b) Thorn's explanation of added value (see the balance sheet and profit and loss account on pages 36 and 37)

Source: Thorn Electrical Industries Special Report for Employees 1978

Our £55m taxes could pay for one of the following...

The taxes (as shown in the Profit and Loss account on page 37) comprise both current and deferred tax. If they were to be paid in full they could be used to finance any one of these.

2 Hospitals

60 000 old age pensions for 1 year

Child benefit for 1 year
for 450 000 children

180 Primary schools

26 Miles of motorway

Thorn's added value included £55m to be paid in taxes. This is what it would buy

Source: Thorn Electrical Industries Special Report for Employees 1978

A delicate balance

The extract from the Thorn company report (facing page) highlights another aspect of the role that industry of all kinds — manufacturing, retailing and commercial; independent and state-owned — plays in modern society.

It is not only supplying the material goods and services we enjoy (some people may think we could well do with a few less of these anyway), but through corporation tax, value added tax, employer's contributions, etc. it also finances the social security benefits, education, the national health service, defence, local authority housing and much more.

In 1977 government expenditure on such services was £54 480m, including £13 213m on social security benefits, £7853m on education of all kinds and £6730m on the health service.

In that year the government received

- £17 631.9m from personal taxes
- £3046.1m from corporation tax on company profits
- £12 091m from indirect taxes such as VAT
- £9453m from national insurance contributions from employees and employers.

During the same year 87.1 per cent of our total working population was working in industry of one form or another (the remainder being unemployed or employed in government services such as the health service, central government and the forces), and almost one-third of all employees work in manufacturing companies. Industry's contribution to our gross domestic product (GDP) in 1977 was £109 116m. The table below shows the comparative levels of contribution to GDP by various different types of industry for 1976.

Gross Domestic Product by industry*
(at current prices)

	1976	
	£m	%
Agriculture, forestry and fishing	3 116	2.8
Mining and quarrying	2 458	2.3
Manufacturing	30 464	27.9
Construction	7 793	7.1
Gas, electricity and water	3 905	3.6
Transport	6 624	6.1
Communications	3 691	3.4
Distributive trades	10 379	9.5
Insurance, banking and finance	7 717	6.2

Source: National Income and Expenditure 1966–76.
* Before provision for depreciation but after deducting stock appreciation.

Discussion

Without the money received from employees and employers, and the contribution of industry to our GDP, from where would the income come to pay for the old age pensions, unemployment, maternity and child benefits, schools and hospitals on which society depends?

It is not a straightforward question to answer as it is bound up with a mass of complex, interrelated economic factors. However, it is difficult to see how without a complete upheaval of society as we know it we can continue to improve the benefits received without correspondingly increasing the productive base which supports them.

Industry and government

One further aspect of the relationship between industry and the society in which it operates deserves special mention. This is the link between companies and the elected government of the day. Business is obviously subject to the laws of the country, as are we all, and these laws control its operation in order, for example, to protect the public from such crimes as fraudulent practice.

A modern government, however, plays a far greater part than simply the administration of the law. It can exert its influence over industry in more subtle ways through taxation, financial assistance, control of prices and wages and sometimes state ownership. The extent to which a government chooses to exercise these powers depend largely on its political persuasion. The critics of intervention say that market forces should be allowed to determine industrial development and decisions on company activities are better made by those within the companies themselves than by organisations far removed from the place of work.

There are several ways in which government influences companies.

Financial assistance

In 1982/83 the government, through the Department of Industry, made available over £2 billion for support to industry. This assistance is used to further specific government objectives, such as encouraging industrial development and employment in areas where unemployment is high; and promoting the development of new technologies like microelectronics, robotics, fibre-optics, computer software, flexible manufacturing methods and advanced office systems.

Help is also given to encourage the growth of new and existing small businesses, for industrial research and development, and research in fields such as aircraft and space technology.

Examples of the amounts available in 1982/83 are
● regional and general industrial support, £534 million
● scientific and technical assistance, £269 million
● support for aerospace, shipbuilding, steel and vehicle manufacture, £606 million.
This does not include nationalised industries.

The government also gives substantial aid to help research, develop and manufacture new products and processes in the information technology field, an amount which is expected to reach £160 million by 1984/85.

Through these various types of financial assistance the government can exert considerable influence over where and in what fields industrial expansion and research and development takes place.

State ownership

The nationalised industries have a strong influence throughout the British economy, dominating as they do the sectors concerned with provision of energy, public transport, post and telecommunications, iron and steel and shipbuilding industries. In 1980 they employed seven per cent of the labour force and so their settlements on matters such as employment and pay can affect other major employers in the country.

Nationalisation came about through the belief that it would bring greater efficiencies and economies of scale; this did not always prove to be the case. The various nationalisation acts gave nationalised industries

their own boards and responsibility for their own businesses, although some limited powers were retained by the government.

In May 1979 there were eighteen nationalised industries. The Conservatives then embarked upon a policy of returning these to the private sector and by mid 1982, seven had either been, or were about to be de-nationalised.

The main motivation for this policy is to increase the efficiency of these industries by allowing them to operate in a competitive market. In addition this reduces the money the government has to raise to support them and, hopefully, enables employees to buy shares and become part owners of the new privately-owned companies.

British Technology Group

The National Research Development Corporation (NRDC) and the National Enterprise Board (NEB) operate together under a common board, as the British Technology Group.

The NEB provides loans of up to £50,000 for the development and exploitation of new technologies, companies operating in assisted areas and small firms. By doing this it encourages other institutions and organisations also to lend the companies money or provide equity finance to add to that provided by the NEB. When it was set up, the NEB was intended to extend public ownership in the companies it supported, but it is now disposing of these holdings to the private sector whenever possible.

The NRDC promotes the development of British inventions. It acts as a channel for exploiting inventions from research paid for by public funds, and also provides finance for innovation by industrial companies wishing to develop their own products or processes. This finance is usually risk capital in the form of joint ventures or equity participation.

Taxation and financial control

Government can influence industrial development and operation through its policy on taxation — its fiscal policy. Taxes on incomes, both earned and from investments, on goods and services, on imports by way of excise duty, on company profits and in the form of capital taxes can all affect industrial development. The way in which revenue is collected, either by direct taxation on earnings or indirect taxation through, for example, value added tax on selected goods, can make a considerable difference to company growth and operation.

In addition, the government has a further source of

financial control, whose effects are less obvious, through regulation of the money supply. The general state of a country is reflected in the exchange rates of its currency which in turn have direct consequences on the internal economy: this will result either in equilibrium or a downward or upward spiral as the case may be.

Export and import control

For a healthy economy a country needs to balance its exports — the foreign exchange earners — with the value of goods it has to buy from abroad, its imports. Imports can be controlled by quotas or, as in the case of some foreign countries, by legislation laying down for example the proportion of components of a machine which have to be manufactured at home. Technical standards, administrative procedures and other 'non-tariff barriers' can also have a significant effect.

In the United Kingdom the government encourages companies to improve their export performance, for example by assistance with schemes to explore new markets or through public recognition of successful effort such as the Queen's Award. Some U.K. imports are subject to customs duty when brought into the country, which increases their price in the shops, although this is not the case with goods from other EEC countries. Since our entry into the Common Market trade has been stimulated with the EEC, rather than with other countries.

Wages and prices

In recent years governments have intervened more actively than before in the region of wages and prices. The Price Commission was established to monitor and control price increases, and in 1977 was given a new power to launch intensive investigation into requests by the bigger companies to put up the prices of their products. The Commission was abolished when the Conservatives came to power in 1979. Price control was intended to keep inflation down, for example, by preventing firms from passing on their employees' pay increases to the consumer without careful consideration. In practice the Price Commission was found not to have a very marked effect on overall prices. Bodies such as the Monopolies and Mergers Commission, the Office of Fair Trading and the Restrictive Trade Practices Court play important parts in ensuring that consumers (whether private individuals or customer companies) are not exploited.

Governments have also attacked the inflation problem by direct intervention in pay settlements. This has taken the form both of a complete pay freeze, when it was only legal to increase a person's salary by

a prescribed sum regardless of job, and of government laying down percentage guidelines on pay awards and using pressure such as the threat of withdrawal of government contracts and financial assistance to persuade firms to settle within these guidelines.

There is a great deal of controversy over whether these methods are helpful in controlling the pay spiral, or whether companies should be left to reach their own agreements with their employees through free collective bargaining with the trade unions.

Industrial relations

The degree to which government should influence the relationship between management and employees is another area on which opinion differs. Legislation already exists (see page 116) which lays down certain requirements that companies must fulfil, including the compulsory disclosure of certain information to their employees. In addition there have been suggestions, notably in the Bullock Report issued in 1977, that the law should make it obligatory for companies to have worker-directors on their boards. There is, however, a strong body of opinion which holds that such decisions should be left to the organisations concerned.

In all these areas government can and does intervene in the affairs of British industry. It may also create significant effects as a result of its ownership of the nation's energy supply, transport and communications services and basic industries such as iron and steel on all of which companies are highly dependent; its grip on the nation's purse strings; its ability to hand out and withdraw massive government contracts and support; and as the instigator of new legislation. In addition both central and local governments' financial and manpower requirements compete against the needs of other users.

The National Economic Development Council

The National Economic Development Council (NEDC or Neddy) was established in 1962 to bring together government, trade unions and employers in an independent body. It is not, therefore, part of government, although it is financed from public funds. Its terms of reference were to examine the economic performance of the nation with particular concern for plans for the future in both the public and private sectors of industry; to consider the obstacles to quicker economic growth, ways of improving efficiency and whether the best use is being made of resources; and to seek agreement on ways of improving economic performance, competitive power and efficiency. The Council meets monthly and is normally chaired by the Chancellor of the Exchequer. A wide range of economic and industrial issues are discussed, the dominant theme being the need to improve the competitive performance of the United Kingdom manufacturing industry.

A network of about fifty industrial committees, also established on a tripartite basis, reports to the NEDC. These cover nearly half our manufacturing output and employment, and export of manufactured goods. The committees identify ways in which industrial performance can be improved, and then try to see these improvements carried out in the companies themselves.

Youth training

With the rising tide of unemployment the government has become increasingly involved in another area of contact with industry — training the young people who will make up the workforce of the future. Through schemes like the Youth Opportunities Program (YOP) and Work Experience Programs, the government has attempted to help industry bridge the gap for school leavers between school and work. In 1982, a new scheme was announced called the Youth Training Scheme, which aims to give training to all 16 and 17 year old school leavers who do not go on to further education, whether they find jobs or not. This scheme is subsidised through the Manpower Services Commission (MSC).

Legislation

In recent years several Acts of Parliament have been passed affecting employees and employers and the relationship between them. This legislation has increased the protection afforded by law to employees and considerably extended their rights. It has also placed a heavy burden on many firms, which find that an increasing proportion of management time is taken up by dealing with the paperwork and administration involved, official inspections and legal procedures.

The following list briefly summarises the main Acts relating to employment passed since 1974.

Health and Safety at Work Act 1974

This provides one system of law to deal with the health and safety of all people at work, and that of the general public affected by work activities. It sets up the Health and Safety Commission which is a body representing both management and unions and is responsible for policy development. The Commission's operational arms are the Health and Safety Executive, which

conducts inspections of factories, mines and such like, and the Employment Medical Advisory Service. The Act imposes a general duty on employers to ensure health, safety and welfare at work, and on employees to take reasonable care for their own and other people's health, safety and welfare. It entitles the trade unions to appoint safety representatives whom the employers are obliged to consult.

Employment Protection Act 1975 and Trade Union and Labour Relations Acts 1974 and 1976

These deal with the collective rights of people at work, and were both amended by the Employment Act 1980. The acts cover areas like union independence and the disclosure, on request, of information by employers to recognised unions. They also ensure consultation with unions on proposed redundancies. They give protection to people on strike; this protection being limited when the employees who strike are not directly involved in the dispute. Similar rules apply to picketing.

Social Security (Pensions) Act 1975

This introduced a new state pension under which there is a 'basic' pension, and an 'additional' pension which is related to earnings and builds up over 20 years. The scheme is linked to prices and makes better provision for widows. It allows employers who provide occupational pension schemes, if these satisfy certain requirements, to contract out of the state scheme. It also gives women equal rights to belong to an occupational pension scheme.

Sex Discrimination Act 1975

This makes it illegal for employers, professional bodies and trade unions to discriminate on the grounds of sex or marital status, except where this can be shown to be a genuine requirement of the job; or to place an advertisement indicating an intention to discriminate.

Race Relations Act 1976

This makes it unlawful to discriminate on the grounds of race, ethnic or national origins, in the fields of employment, education facilities and services, housing and clubs.

Employment Protection (Consolidation) Act 1978

This deals with the rights of individuals on matters such as contracts of employment, periods of notice, time off for union and public duties, maternity leave, unfair dismissal, redundancy payment, and rights not to be penalised for union membership. Employees who feel their rights have been infringed can make a complaint to an industrial tribunal.

1978. In addition, the act gives an employee the right not to be unreasonably excluded from a union where there is a closed shop and it allows for public funds to be used by unions to conduct secret ballots.

Employment Act 1980

This amended the Employment Protection Acts and Trade Union and Labour Relations Acts from 1974 to

The role of Government in industry

The Conservative party view

The Conservative party's industrial policy has three objectives:
- the creation of a climate in which industry can flourish
- positive action to make markets work more freely
- positive stimulation of industry in areas where this is a cost effective use of tax payers money.

The Conservatives' main drive is the fight against inflation. Inflation makes planning for the future hazardous and so delays investment; it sours industrial relations and puts pressure on wage costs; it hampers competition with overseas producers, and it forces up interest rates.

Conservatives believe that to reduce inflation government spending and borrowing must be cut. Also the cost of borrowing money must be kept down to encourage new investment and help people wanting to start their own businesses.

Secondly Conservatives want to improve market efficiency, and with this in mind pay, price, dividend, exchange and hire purchase control have been abolished. Conservatives have a policy of trade union reform — ensuring the balance of negotiating strength between employers and trade unions. They also encourage the labour force to be mobile to make the most of industrial expansion in different areas.

Generally the Conservatives feel that industry is best managed by the industrialists. This said, selective help is offered to certain sectors of industry, for example, small businesses and companies involved in technological developments. Conservatives see a clear Government

role in promoting new products and processes which would otherwise not be developed.

Conservatives also try to make sure that the tax system encourages individuals by making it more worthwhile to work and to work hard, and more worthwhile for companies to invest in their businesses. They also believe in encouraging overseas investors by offering investment incentives and creating a climate attractive to them.

However firm the financial discipline imposed on the state sector of industry, it can never reproduce the effectiveness of the market and competition in increasing efficiency. Yet, improved efficiency in the state sector is crucial to the creation of a better climate for industry. The main aims of Conservative policy on nationalised industries are
- where possible to return them to the private sector
- to reduce the extent of state-owned monopolies
- to improve the efficiency of the remaining nationalised industries
- to ensure that the state is an intelligent purchaser of industry's goods and services.

The overriding aim of Conservative industrial policy is to provide a framework in which the creation of wealth is given every possible encouragement. That is the only way to help the sick, the elderly and the disabled. That is the only way to afford to build decent hospitals and schools. That is the only way in which people can achieve a steady increase in living standards.

The Labour party view

The story of British industry has not been a story of success. Over the years we have seen the decline of leading industries and the decay of once thriving economic centres. Overall, our industries have failed to match our competitors in their level of investment, their speed of innovation and their ability to adapt to changing world conditions. The monetarist policies of the Conservatives have accelerated this structural decline. Four million jobs have been lost in industry since 1966, and one and a half million of these went between 1979 and 1982. This decline is a consequence of the way industry is organised and run.

Decision making in the economy has become concentrated in fewer and fewer hands. No more than a hundred large companies — almost all of them multinationals — control 40 per cent of manufacturing output and over half our exports. The increasing concentration of ownership and control in industry is matched by a similar trend among banks and financial institutions, whose power has grown enormously in recent years. Crucial economic decisions have been taken without any accountability to workers and the community at large. Many of these decisions are responsible for the mass unemployment and industrial decline whose effects we are now suffering.

Labour's programme of expansion provides a framework for industrial regeneration. Within a framework of a growing economy, Labour's policy is to introduce a coherent industrial strategy to rebuild the shattered industrial base and reverse the spiral of decline. Central to this industrial strategy are proposals on economic planning and industrial democracy. These proposals are set out in a joint report with the TUC, and the key points are given below.

Labour's industrial strategy has two fundamental objectives: to make industry more efficient and to make it more democratic. They judge efficiency not just by levels of productivity, but by the ability of industry to meet the needs of society. By democracy, is meant the accountability of industry both to its workers through structures of industrial democracy, and to the community as a whole through a system of planning. The key to the socialist approach is that Labour believe these twin objectives — efficiency and democracy — are inseparable. They believe that our economy will remain inefficient as long as the use of resources is uncoordinated and the real skills and potential of working people are suppressed by their exclusion from decision-making.

The problem is to reconcile a planned approach to the regeneration of industry with the full democratic participation at enterprise, sector and national levels. Labour's view is that the development of collective bargaining and joint control is the best means of ensuring that decision-making at all these levels is accountable to workers and the society as a whole. A high priority for Labour is the introduction of an Economic Planning and Industrial Democracy Bill to put these proposals into effect.

The key elements in Labour's socialist industrial strategy are:

- Economic planning both to coordinate economic recovery and to revitalise industry, so that the pattern of output corresponds more closely to social priorities
- Industrial democracy to develop workers' influence over the management of industry and public services, and to extend the principle of accountability to every level of planning
- Common ownership through an extension of public enterprise, the return of denationalised assets to the public sector, the creation of co-operatives and other means, to bring greater collective control over the development of industry and a fair distribution of the wealth that is generated

- Regulation of the financial system to ensure that it provides for the financial needs of industry and government.

To sum up, Labour's view is that planning must be linked to a powerful extension of industrial democracy.

The Liberal Party view

The Liberal party has a considerable heritage in its approach to industrial strategy, much of which is contained in its classic 'Yellow Book' on Britain's Industrial Future, published in 1928 and compiled by a group of distinguished authors who included Lloyd George, Maynard Keynes, Herbert Samuel, Seebohm Rowntree and several others.

The Party has, however, retained perhaps more than any other Party, a flexibility in the handling of current industrial problems, simply because it has by and large kept itself free from constraints and obligations derived not from social philosophy nor even from the momentum of events, but from pressure groups representing variously labour, capital or sectional interests.

Unlike Labour, for instance, the Liberal Party has no 'Clause 4' commitment to nationalisation. They are not dependent on the unions for their Party funds nor do block votes determine their Party policies, leadership or electoral strategy.

Unlike the Conservatives, they do not have obligations to business pressure groups, nor do their funds derive in any major way from large companies or Employers' Federations.

Their attitude to nationalisation and public ownership, which they would very sharply restrict, reflects their concern for industrial efficiency, for individual initiative and enterprise, and for human and community relations rather than extremes of political dogma.

For the same reason they fight continuously for the small and medium enterprise, and are constantly vigilant against abuses of monopoly power exercised through labour, capital or technology.

In enterprises of every kind, both public and private, Liberals seek to pass effective decision-making from the centre down to regional and local

management units. At the level of the shop floor in particular they are advocates of joint consultation through representative Workplace Councils: whilst within the Board Room they favour the introduction of employee-directors drawn from an electorate composed of all employees of the company with full access to papers and with the full rights and responsibilities of directors under the Companies Act. On the other hand the Liberal Party opposed the recommendations of the Bullock Report on employee-directors, with its concept of workers directors nominated to the Board as representatives of their Unions. This they saw as a recipe for continuous and highly dangerous conflicts of interest at Board level.

From this same desire to avoid confrontation policy comes the great emphasis of the Liberal Party on proportional representation. For they consider that the rejection of 'adversary politics' through electoral reform offers to industry the promise of that stability and continuity of policy without which industrial investment is always difficult and quite often foolhardy.

It is the object, therefore, of the Liberal Party to establish within the UK a lively, innovative and successful industrial scene, composed as far as possible, of small or medium sized independent enterprises with the minimum of Government intervention and with the fullest possible personal involvement of all who engage in manufacturing, commercial or service enterprises.

They are, however, conscious that successful business itself poses certain social and moral dilemmas which their Party, perhaps more than any other, has sought to reconcile.

(1) Business activities can create wide anomolies of money, influence and power which can themselves be the source of considerable social unrest and inequity. That is why Liberals seek widespread participation both in ownership and profits and give every possible encouragement through fiscal and other measures to co-operative and common ownership ventures. They are also advocates of prices and incomes policy as a means of keeping inflation

under control whilst at the same time ensuring equitable rewards both for individuals and for companies.

(2) The products of industry can exact an unacceptable social cost to our towns and countryside and our natural resources, and to the health and well-being of human and animal life. Liberals are particularly vigilant to minimise industrial hazards to health and safety and wasteful use of natural resources.

(3) Liberals are in favour of small and medium size firms, but they realise that modern technology is vastly expensive, particularly in R & D and in marketing. They therefore accept the need for Government help, particularly in pump-priming of technological research and in marketing, particularly in assisting market-entry overseas. They also recognise the continuing contribution of the large multi-national companies, but call for a strict enforcement of international conventions and agreements on monopolies and mergers, and on restrictive practices in marketing, administration, pricing, patents and other forms of technology transfer.

(4) As the historic Party of Free Trade, Liberals aim to maximise the flow of goods and services throughout the World. They welcome the development of area trading groups and the creation of common markets for trade promotion. They see such groupings, however, not as inward looking protective devices, but as a means of securing a better balance of negotiating power for different areas of the World, in a common desire to reduce tariff and non-tariff barriers to trade and to secure true reciprocal access for all countries to the markets of the World.

Finally, the Liberal party believes that wherever possible the needs of the consumer and of the public interest should be served by voluntary codes of practice imposed by business itself and negotiated in consultation with Government and their customers. But in the ultimate it is for Parliament to reflect the needs of the public for protection and representation, and Liberals, therefore, support (and would see strengthened) the Office of Fair Trading and Monopolies and Mergers Commission. They also favour direct representation on Public Boards and regret their removal from the newly created Post Office and Telecommunications Boards.

In short the protection of the individual and the subordination of the State are cardinal principles in industry as elsewhere in the economy. But from time to time the size and complexity of modern industry, together with the power of advertising, swings the pendulum against the consumer and the public interest, and it is there, regretfully, that Liberals acknowledge that the State itself must step in.

The Social Democratic party view

Social Democrats believe that industry can only thrive if Government provides it with the right economic and industrial relations background which helps it to compete effectively both at home and abroad. But even if sustained growth in the economy was bought about by a steady reflation backed up by an anti-inflationary incomes policy and a better climate of industrial relations through democratising and de-politicising the trade unions and by introducing industrial democracy, Social Democrats still think it necessary to have a quite clear industrial strategy.

What sort of strategy would a Social Democratic Government seek to adopt?

It is felt to be essential to put the long and sterile debate about ownership behind us. The incessant concentration on nationalisation and de-nationalisation has done much damage to industry through the uncertainty it has created and has hindered the development of a creative industrial policy based on a genuine partnership between Government and industry. It is such a partnership which Social Democrats would seek to establish, within the context of the mixed economy.

The main aim of such a partnership would be to enable industry to adapt to the demands of home and world markets as speedily and effectively as possible. Since industry itself is best able to judge, and much of it is well able to meet the challenge of international competition, the Government's role should be a limited one. It should help companies to develop and adapt from time to time by providing specific assistance to fund some of the costs of adjustment and taking general measures — for example, to encourage training or innovation — which would help foster a flourishing business environment.

But although generally Social Democrats would rely on market pressures to induce industry to adapt and make the necessary changes, it is felt that a positive though limited industrial strategy is essential to bring about improved industrial performance. It is felt to be just as wrong to seek an uncomprising 'hands off' approach, leaving everything to the market as it is to go for the 'Government knows best' state planning and control route. The Social Democrat approach, therefore, is based upon four major principles.

Firstly, industry must be the top priority of the Government. Meeting the needs of industry should be recognised as the top priority in the formulation and implementation of *all* Government policies. This means that fiscal policy and the orientation of the educational system must bear in mind the needs of industry just as much as Government policies on public purchasing, funds for investment, assistance for R & D and training and other policies directly affecting industry.

Second, Government should have an industrial strategy not a grand plan. This will involve a gradual development of policy within each specific sector, informed by an overall view of the sort of developments to be encouraged. Changes in the pattern of industry would then be encouraged by a variety of measures some of which would be available to all firms and sectors, but also inevitably some will be available to only certain sectors and certain firms. This selective approach may at times seem harsh and unfair but Social Democrats see no alternative if they are to succeed and not waste public resources.

Third, the strategy must be formulated and implemented on the basis of a partnership between the different interests involved. The achievement of consensus on the need for industrial change and the broad outlines of that change would be vital if the groups affected by change are to accept it. The concept of partnership is a key element in our whole approach to industry.

Fourth, the Government should seek to work with the market and not against it. Where UK industry is competing effectively without Government aid, there should be no Government involvement. Support should, however, be available for innovation and risk-taking in those businesses in which there are opportunities for British firms to grow and become internationally competitive.

But it means equally, that whilst intervention may be justified to halt or reverse long-term and gradual decline in mature industries before it becomes too late, Government must not become locked into continuing, major support for fundamentally uncompetitive industries which have no hope for the future. Government does, nevertheless, have a role to provide assistance in managing the withdrawal from industries in irreversible decline.

These are powerful and far-reaching principles, affecting the general orientation of Government policy, bearing directly on many individual areas of policy, and requiring important changes in the machinery of Government to be made effective. Social Democrats have also made detailed proposals outlining the changes in the machinery of Government that will be necessary and the concrete ways in which the principles would be implemented.

Discussion

Through these articles we have seen the approach of the main political parties to the part government should play in industry. In the light of these and any other relevant material you can gather, consider what form this role should take in Britain. You might look at the following areas.

(1) Should the government exercise legal restraint on pay? If not, should it bring pressure to bear on companies to keep wage increases within prescribed limits, or should it allow employers and employees to arrive at their own agreements on pay through free collective bargaining? What are the advantages and disadvantages of the three approaches?

(2) To what extent is it desirable for the government to control factors such as prices and imports?

(3) How much of a say should the government have in the way companies are run?

(4) How big a part should the law play in controlling the relationship between the employer and the employee? What are the advantages and disadvantages of having legislation covering aspects such as unfair dismissal, discrimination, health and safety and so on? Would it be possible to achieve the same ends through voluntary control by individual firms?

(5) Should the government exert influence over the way companies carry out their communication, consultation and employee participation? Would it be a good thing if legislation were passed to make firms have worker/directors on their boards?

(6) Should the government be in a position to dispense public money to support flagging industries and preserve jobs?

Work and the Future

14

This book has been about British industry as it is today, but what of the future?

We have looked at the patterns which industry and commerce have developed over many decades. Much of this tradition will remain in the years to come but, inevitably, there will be changes.

The last few years have seen a huge increase in unemployment. World recession, in some cases out dated factories and designs, and the introduction of new technology, combined to put some three million people out of work by the middle of 1982.

This has resulted in a new way of thinking about the future. No longer can every school leaver expect to walk into a job. Governments are concentrating on youth training to prepare young people for work, and for a rewarding life if they cannot find the job of their choice.

Competition for jobs has increased a hundred fold, and successful applicants are better qualified than ever before.

Opinions on what the future holds in store are as diverse as they are many. Authorities differ on the route British industry is going to take and how we can stem the tide of unemployment. Many see the future lying with the small business. New businesses are springing up all over the country and young people themselves, unable to find satisfaction in a difficult job market, are starting up on their own.

Others feel that the work that is available will have to be shared. They propose shorter working weeks, job sharing and early retirement as ways of distributing the work available amongst as many people as possible.

Increased leisure time has obvious attractions, as does the fact that wage earners may be able to spend more time with their families and growing children. We come up against financial constraints, however, as those sharing a job would not probably be able to live on a shared wage and might have to be partly supported by the state.

Without doubt certain sectors of our industry, notably manufacturing and heavy engineering, are contracting, while there is expansion in the fields of high technology and the leisure industries. Our workforce will have to be continually trained and retrained to be flexible enough to make the most of the opportunities in expanding areas, as they are forced to move away from the more traditional areas of employment.

Many of us are suspicious of forecasts of drastic changes to society. Human nature does not change overnight, nor do human needs, and while those needs are there society will see that they are filled. The silicon chip may be the biggest technological advance since the wheel, but we have coped with the wheel — where should we be without it? — and there is no reason why today's new technology should not be seen to represent a challenge to British industry not a death toll, with increasing, exciting opportunities for those joining it.

Meanwhile we have, perhaps, reached a crossroads and the way we now turn may play a very important part in the shape of things to come.

The following articles present four views on aspects of what the future holds in store, and what directions are open to us.

The first is by Tom Stonier, Professor of the School of Science and Society at the University of Bradford, who describes what he sees as our move into a 'post-industrial' society.

Then there are the views of two sixth formers, James Goode and Nicholas Vineall, recent winners of the Observer Whitbread essay competition, who set out their ideas on how our working lives and society might develop and adapt to unemployment, and how the introduction of new technology will change our industry.

The final article presents the viewpoint of John Garnett, director of The Industrial Society, an organisation whose members include industrial and commercial companies, trade unions, nationalised industries, central and local government departments and employers' associations, and whose aim is to promote the fullest involvement of people in their work, in order to increase both the effectiveness and profitability of the organisation and the satisfaction of the individual.

The emerging post-industrial society

Tom Stonier

At the beginning of the eighteenth century nearly 92 per cent of the labour force worked on farms to feed the other 8 per cent: agriculture and not industry was the major mode of production. Industry, it was believed, was a parasite of the agricultural society.

During the nineteenth century industrial activity proved itself capable of not only generating tremendous amounts of wealth, but draining labour away from the farms on an enormous scale. Today, only 3 per cent of the labour force work on farms to feed the rest of the population. This was the result of technology providing tools such as tractors, fertilisers and hybrid seeds, which made exploitation of the land so much more efficient.

The invention of the steam engine established a new major mode of production. This new form of power coupled to existing machinery magnified their capabilities many times. Locomotives, power looms and farm machinery all added to the shift of labour from the farms to the factories, as the industrial society developed.

Today a new shift is taking place. And again it is the result of a new technology. In Germany and Japan large sections of automobile assembly lines operate virtually devoid of human hands. Information machines, originally called computers, have been linked to existing machinery as was the steam engine. The result is the displacement of labour as factory machines are no longer manned by 'machine operatives' but by the new information machines. A welding 'robot' can be 'taught' by a master welder for instance, to attach the wings to a car. After that it will perform its function

24 hours a day, 365 days a year. Backed up by information machines which inventory stock and handle orders, many middle-line management jobs will be obviated as well. Equally startling will be the displacement in offices: typing pools can be cut in half, and achieve an overall 300 per cent increase of output. Corporation investment in this case is zero, since the microprocessors can be bought out of the savings on staff. By early in the next century it will probably take only 10 per cent of the labour force to produce all our material needs, ranging from food and clothing to automobiles and appliances.

Just as it was wrong to assume that agriculture was the only road to societal wealth, it is equally wrong to believe that manufacturing industry is the final producer of wealth. Both agriculture and industry succeeded and were displaced by organised information in the form of new technologies. And it is in the field of information that 'post-industrial' society will find its new source of wealth. This does not mean that there will be no industry, just as the industrial revolution did not mean an end to agriculture. However, the labour requirements will be radically different. The dominant feature of 'post-industrialised' industry is that it will be run by highly educated engineers coupled to advanced, highly-productive robotised manufacturing systems.

The majority of people will be working in the service sector. They will be employed by government in the health and social services, and in particular, in education. A massive expansion of education would fulfil a society's need

for the most important single resource a 'post-industrial' economy requires — knowledge. The fertile plains of Europe became productive about a thousand years ago as a result of the deep plough technology and Europe emerged as the most powerful area on earth. A few years ago, North Sea oil became a resource as the result of technology where it was previously inaccessible. As a result of growing knowledge new technologies can be developed to uncover and exploit what are presently 'non-resources'. An excess of coal and wave power, coastal fish farming and single cell protein production, once efficiently exploited, means that Britain can become a net exporter of food and power even after North Sea oil runs out.

The most pressing problem confronting British society is how to effect the orderly transfer of labour from the manufacturing to the knowledge industries. This could be accomplished by a massive expansion of education subsidised by the government. It would create millions of jobs, keep the young off the labour market and in education, allow the obsolete and the redundant to be retrained, prepare students to face the complex society of the next century, and would help in creating new industries on which the wealth of a nation depends. Knowledge of how to make resources out of non-resources such as an excess of coal and wave power, coastal fish farming, and single cell protein production, can only be achieved through education coupled to research and development. Such an investment not only represents the guarantee of a rich future in social terms, but also in economic terms.

How could society adapt to a high level of permanent unemployment?

James Goode

At a time when unemployment soars, when old economic remedies have been tried and failed and people struggle to maintain their standard of living, many are now confronted with the prospect of permanent leisure. The 'Technological Revolution' will, according to some, bring widespread and permanent unemployment to industrial Britain.

But will it?

I hope to show that while the search for traditional full employment is a dangerous and misconceived one, there is a trend which points the way to a future of abundant work, and abundant leisure: a trend which challenges our assumptions about how, where and even why we work, and in the process changes the meaning of work itself. For we are about to see the emergence of the New Work: the result of a social and economic revolution which will alter our perception of industrial civilisation's basic institution – The Market.

Until the Industrial Revolution the market economy was, of course, very primitive: what market activity there was usually took the form of simple barter, and was almost always on a small scale. Generally people produced goods not to exchange, but to use themselves. A typical family unit would grow and make just enough to keep itself going, with any small surplus being sold or bartered. In other words, pre-industrial societies were structured around a fused economy, where producer and consumer were one and the same.

The Industrial Revolution tore that society apart. The economy was split into a production side and a consumption side, and we came to regard ourselves as producers and consumers.

It is that split between production and consumption, the split which created an expanding exchange network to connect the two, the split which structured government and institution, which created a materialist ethic and changed our conception of work and leisure. The gap between our existence as producers and as consumers is now being bridged. It is only through an understanding of the immense historical

significance of this change, which transcends all conventional political boundaries, that we can design coherent policies on employment for the present, and for the future.

What we are experiencing is not, as has been suggested, a shift towards a 'service society', but a shift towards a 'self-service' society. We have actually seen, with the exception of education and health, a substantial drop in the consumption of services over the last twenty years: more and more, people are 'doing-it-themselves'. As Dr Jonathon Gershuny in his book *After Industrial Society* points out:

> "instead of buying services, households are actually INVESTING in durable goods which allow them, as final consumers, to produce services for themselves."

Witness increasing sales of cars, domestic appliances, home video and computer systems, and the phenomenal growth of 'D.I.Y'.

As a result of this we could begin to see the emergence of the home-centered society, a phenomenon already appearing in America: more work done at home, often via computer; more education based at home; and through such information systems as Prestel, the ability to order goods direct from the manufacturer, direct from home.

Implications of this development for employment are tremendous. It would not only mean less commuting to work, or more flexible working hours. We could eventually see industrial processes responding to direct instruction from the home or office computer, reducing the need for labour in between, and further blurring the distinction between producer and consumer.

Within such a framework our whole attitude to work would be dramatically changed. More people could be involved in production of goods and services for their own use, as well as in production for exchange.

The concept of the Welfare State could be stood on its head, so that instead of providing relief as a last resort every person could be paid a basic minimum income by the government,

making part-time lower-paid work in the exchange economy more attractive. People would therefore top-up their minimum income by working part-time in the market (production for exchange) sector of the economy, while doing unpaid community work/education/ recreation/housework in the 'production for use' sector

In this situation the rigid division created by industrial society separating producer from consumer would largely disappear, and with it the distinction between work and leisure. The idea of 'education for leisure' in its narrow, specialised sense becomes irrelevant. We would live in a society where everybody was at work (i.e. making a positive contribution to society) whichever sector of the economy this was in.

There would be no unemployment.

But there are real problems with this scenario (apart from the obvious political difficulties), and they are basically two-fold.

Firstly, where would the money for a minimum income scheme come from? Certainly almost all the resources used for the present welfare system, a re-distribution of existing government expenditure and possibly increases in taxation would meet costs. Though the scheme is extremely costly, it is difficult to imagine a realistic alternative. People will not readily accept permanent leisure, subsidised by the State, while a minority are in full-time employment and earn a good deal more money. The distinction between employed and unemployed would be stronger than ever, and there would inevitably be resentment. The proposed scheme points the way to a potentially exciting future, filled with myriad opportunties for rewarding work and satisfying leisure.

The second, and to my mind more important problem is how we prepare people for change. How could we begin to adapt to the New Work? First, we must be honest. We must not try to ressurect obsolete industrial concepts in a world which is moving rapidly into post-industrialism. Those politicians who promise a return to full employment know, possibly better than anyone else, that in a world competing viciously for resources and markets the new labour-saving technologies are bound to be adopted.

And despite official optimism it is highly unlikely that enough new industries will spring up to absorb the jobless — for it would mean finding completely new products for completely new markets. Replacement products — as in the case of digital versus conventional watches — only transfer jobs from one factory to another: they create no new ones. In fact, any major new developments one can dream up, any marvellous new products that our

society could ever realistically wish for, almost all are in some way replacements, or technically sophisticated substitutes for what exists now. The age of the ever-expanding market is coming to an end. We have built our world. All we can do now is update it.

This is the situation which today confronts our leaders, and it is they who must have the courage and the vigour to prepare people for change. It is industrial and scientific and political leaders who must give people an awareness of encouraging possibilities for the future, and make suggestions as to how we might overcome the difficulties which

are sure to arrive during the transitional phase.

We appear to be on the brink of the most tremendous economic and social transformation since the Industrial Revolution. New forms of government, new institutions and attitudes are destined to be created around a new concept of man's role in society. The sooner we stop applying obsolete industrial remedies to emerging post-industrial problems, the sooner we can set about structuring the New Work, in the New Age.

Industry and the challenge of the silicon chip

Nicholas Vineall

The wheel, the deep plough, the steam engine, the production line, all bear witness to man's insatiable appetite for automation. At irregular intervals an invention or discovery provides fresh impetus for industry. Often the revolutionary innovation comes hand in hand with threatened revolution, for example social disturbances such as the Luddite riots of the late eighteenth century. Workers, anxious for their livelihood, fear for their jobs and hit out at the machines that threaten to put them out of work. Yet always it transpired that the number of jobs destroyed was vastly exceeded by the number of jobs created.

The most recent technological advance has come in the form of a break through in the world of electronics. In the early nineteen fifties, bulky electronic components like radio valves and thermionic diodes were superseded by far smaller semi-conductor devices such as transistors. Recently, the miniaturisation process has been carried a stage further. Today, one hundred thousand transistors and resistors can be condensed on to a single, tiny chip of silicon. Yet more significant than the dramatic decrease in size, that has transformed large circuit boards to minute integrated circuits, is the corresponding decrease in cost and increase in complexity and reliability.

The introduction of the silicon chip has been described as a phenomenal

breakthrough representing a major leap towards complete automation. Some would say that this overdramatizes the event, and that proximity to the scene is distorting perspective. On the other hand, the chip is intrinsically different from previous innovations. It is not analogous to, to take but two examples, the introduction of the lathe or the numerically controlled machine, for the chip cannot conceivably produce as much labour as it destroys.

The over-riding capacity of the chip for destroying jobs is due to its extreme versatility. It has myriad applications because its function is one of control. This is a totally new departure, for in the past the products of science used in industry have known application only as tools; as horses to carry the load of man's tasks, yet always with man holding the reins. For the first time science has provided a way for man to be almost totally replaced by a semi-automatic brain — the integrated circuit. Thus primary, secondary and tertiary industry is affected by the microprocessor.

The national coal board is soon to introduce a new type of drilling head to work at the coal face. At present one man steers the machine whilst another calls out instructions, whilst being covered in coal dust and the water needed to cool the face. In the future the machine will be automatic, main-

taining the four inches of coal required to be left as a ceiling to the shaft without any human participation.

In manufacturing industry the chip has been quick to make its presence felt. National cash registers have halved their workforce since the microprocessor became available. At Wolfsburg in Germany, Volkswagen has one production line 'manned' entirely by seventy robots.

Word processing is currently revolutionising the newspaper industry. Journalists can now type directly into a visual display unit, and then edit, paragraph and amend what they have written. When they are satisfied, the finished article is converted to print automatically.

Word processors and increasingly faster and more complex data transmission systems will undoubtedly have a profound effect on office and clerical work. As the roles of secretaries and clerks become redundant so too will the clerks and secretaries themselves. Siemens foresees computerised equipment carrying out forty per cent of the office jobs at present performed manually. The French banks suspect that their workforce will be thirty per cent smaller ten years from now.

In certain applications, the chip has altered not only a manufacturing process but also the product itself. Adding machines of fifteen years ago have now been totally superseded by electronic calculators. Digital watches, accurate, cheap and reliable, have wrought havoc in the Swiss and German quality watch industries. The workforce of the latter has fallen to eighteen thousand from thirty-two thousand only nine years ago.

Thus the chip threatens widespread unemployment. But the chip also, indeed therefore, offers an unprecedented potential for improving our lives. Now at last is an opportunity to replace the tedium of many dull, monotonous repetitive tasks by increased employment in service industries: nursing, care and education and also in research of all kinds. There can be much more time for leisure and enjoyment generally.

Herein lies the challenge of the silicon chip. It is a challenge to everyone, but industry must lead the way. Introduction of the microprocessor must be carefully considered. Industry must to some extent overcome its monetarist, profit-making motives. There is no necessity for self-effacing altruism, only forward-planning and farsightedness. If chip-controlled automation is suddenly selectively applied to one industry with no provision for those put out of work, there is little doubt that neo-ludditism will be the result. Undoubtedly, society is laying a great burden on the shoulders of industry. The reaction of industry, particularly the large employers, must be a responsible one. The future of society is probably more directly in the hands of industry than it has ever been before. Industry must rise to the challenge of the silicon chip. The fear of, and reaction to, job-destroying automation has been highlighted by the disputes at Times Newspapers. Without careful redistribution of remaining labour, without the creation of new jobs in service industries, and without education towards a new outlook — enjoying life rather than making money out of it — without a move away from the protestant work ethic and the equation of work with influence and happiness and of unemployment with misery and deprivation, society will be overburdened by the shock of lost working hours and the increased leisure time at man's disposal.

The chip may not be fully effective for another fifty years, but its challenge is with us now. It is a challenge to industry. It is an exciting challenge that must be taken up. It is to realize the potential of the chip whilst maintaining a social conscience. The future of society rests upon industry's response to the challenge of the silicon chip.

The challenge of the future

John Garnett

The challenge for future generations is to call forth the gifts of people in order to create a better world for all to live in. To do this, we need to find ways of using the world's resources more sparingly and with greater ingenuity.

Previous generations have spent too much time debating how to distribute available wealth; we have failed to find ways of creating more and, as a result, there is now less to divide. In this country, we are already consuming every year more than £1500 per family of four more than we are creating. We must start to pay our way so that we can do more for the old and the young, so that we can build better hospitals and schools and so that we can assist the less developed countries in their struggle for economic growth.

Such real achievements will not be secured by passing political resolutions but rather by harnessing the gifts of people at work to create what is needed.

The opportunities for the future are enormous: for example, the advantages of new technological inventions can benefit mankind immensely if we can find ways of harnessing this technology responsibly.

Semi-conductor technology can create new products (pocket calculators, tele-text); replace existing products (mechanical watches); extend the capabilities of products (programmed instructions for washing machines); change production and office methods (robots and word processing); and change the way in which products are designed (computer-aided design).

All these qualities, coupled with the difficulty of understanding how such devices work, makes this new technology a natural candidate for suspicious and Luddite-like hostility. And yet, this technology is a potential source of great benefit.

There are tremendous opportunities for manufacturing industry if we think in positive terms; we can introduce a wide range of new wealth-creating industries with new employment prospects and a whole series of new technical products.

Our rate of future economic growth will largely depend on our ability to accept rapid change, and on our ability to persuade others to accept change, to learn new skills and retrain to a high level.

We cannot reject the future since we depend for our national livelihood on competing successfully in the markets of the world. Either we grasp the initiative or we do not compete at all. If our competitors are boosting their productivity and reducing their labour costs, we have no option but to do the same if we wish to maintain employment and improve our standard of living.

But, if we are to play a valuable part in their new world, we need to understand the vital importance of involving people in their work. We must experience the frustrations and the lack of communication which exist throughout factories and offices. We need to develop our own powers of leadership in every walk of life, whether at school or at work. Only then shall we discover how working life can be made better for people, and how people can be more effective in what they do.

There will always be worries and difficulties in the future, but we can overcome these if we see every problem as a new challenge. We must also recognise the importance of industry and commerce so that it is as worthy to become a builder and build houses as it is to join the local authority and allocate them.

The future lies with those who realise that there is nothing so worthy as to give a true and honest service to our fellow men by making the products that people need.

Discussion

These four articles together with the wealth of argument, comment and crystal ball-gazing occurring daily in the press and on the radio and television, should provide sufficient material for a discussion on the direction which you think the future development of British industry should take and how this would affect you as individuals. You might conside the following questions.

(1) Is unemployment inevitably going to continue to rise? How can we best tackle the problem that unemployment, even at its present levels can bring? List all the approaches available to us and consider each on its merits, bearing in mind its effects on other aspects of the economy and society.

(2) What can you do to increase your chances of getting a job you will enjoy? If you are competing with a hundred other people for one job, how can you convince an employer that you are the one to choose? How can you find out more about possible careers and the qualifications and experience you need to go into them?

(3) Do you accept the view that our material needs are becoming satiated, or do you see these needs, or wants, increasing as society becomes more and more sophisticated?

(4) How can we ensure that our industry and commerce is ready to respond to the challenges which the future may bring, so that we can become increasingly competitive in international markets?

Class activity

Starting your own business — exercise and discussion

Nowadays more and more people, sometimes even straight from school, are considering starting their own businesses. Some have been unsuccessful in their search for employment, while others have received redundancy money which gives them a long-awaited chance to start up on their own. The rewards of self employment can be great, but the hazards many.

In this exercise we ask you to think about the problems and challenges of starting a business and how you would go about it. Some of you may come up with ideas which you can actually put into practice as part of a school project, in the holidays or at home.

The qualities you need

People who start and successfully run their own businesses are often called entrepreneurs. Make a list of what you think are the six most important qualities needed by someone wanting to set up on their own. Put the list in order of importance.

Does anyone in your group meet all these requirements?

The advantages and disadvantages of becoming self-employed

Listed here are some of the advantages and disadvantages of self employment. Decide which would be the most significant to you and put them in order of importance.

Do you think that for you the advantages would outweigh the disadvantages, or vice versa?

Disadvantages
- unpredictable and irregular income, at least at first
- working long hours with no paid holidays
- taking risks, often with your own money
- having to live with the strain of wondering where the next order is coming from and whether you are making the right decisions some of which may affect the whole future of the business
- having to spend a great deal of time on administration, tax and VAT returns and lots of paper work
- receiving no company pension.

Advantages
- you are your own boss, making your own decisions
- you can be involved with all aspects of running the business
- you have the satisfaction of having built a business if you succeed
- potentially you can make more money than as an employee
- you will seldom be bored — you don't have time to be.

Skills and products

Many of the people who make a success of their own business start in a very small way. They have a skill or hobby which they feel they can sell and they begin to test out the market in the evenings or at weekends. See how many of your group have a skill or an idea they think could be exploited commercially. Amongst you there may be a potential textile designer, motor mechanic or someone who could run a word processing or typing service from home.

If you can think of a potential product or service, consider how you would go about setting up a company to sell it. Discuss the answers to the following questions and prepare an action plan for establishing your hypothetical business:

(1) Who could you contact for advice? Is there anyone you know who knows about the market you would be going into? What professional or government organisations are available in your area to help small businesses?

(2) Describe the product in detail. How could you market it? Who would buy it and where do they live? How can it be made? How many similar products would you be competing with? Why would yours be better?

(3) What experience do you have as individuals or as a group which would help you set up and run your business? What experience do you lack? Where could you find this experience?

(4) How could your product be made or your service organised, and how much could you sell?

(5) Where would your business be based? At home, perhaps, or in an office, factory or shop? How could you find such premises and what would they cost?

(6) How many people would you need to run the business with you? Could you manage alone to start with?

(7) What would it cost to make the product or produce the service, both fixed and variable costs? How much would you have to charge?

(8) How would you structure your business, as a sole trader, partnership or limited company?

(9) How much money do you think you would need to raise? How do you calculate this figure? Where would you go for the money?

Putting ideas into practice

So far you have only looked at a theoretical business you might one day like to run. You could also do a more detailed project on a product which you could make as a group while you are still at school. Your product might, for example, be chocolate Easter eggs, wax candles or Christmas and birthday cards, the materials for which are readily available.

Try setting up a management team and forecasting how much it would cost you to produce, say, one hundred cards and how much you could sell them for. How could you sell them?

You could expand this into a project for running a real business from your school or college and see whether you can make it profitable. Alternatively you might try simulating the running of the business on a computer to see whether you have the makings of a successful entrepreneur and whether your ideas have a chance of standing up to the test of the real competitive business world.

Other Activities and Bibliography

A book of this sort cannot possibly cover all aspects of industry. There are several ways in which students and classes can find further information on those aspects which interest them. Listed here are some suggestions about obtaining additional material, useful organisations and a few of the ways in which students can find out more about life in industry.

Resource material

Careers Research and Advisory Council
CRAC produces some very useful material, including business games written specially for schools, a production game and business experience case studies. A catalogue is available from the Publications Department, Hobsons Press, Bateman Street, Cambridge CB2 1LZ.

Also available is a list of business simulations and case studies produced by other organisations which are suitable for use in schools. The list gives the price and from where they can be obtained.

The Industrial Society
The Society produces several film strips on different aspects of industry, some of which have been used as a basis for case studies in this book. There are also booklets on relevant subjects which can be obtained from the Publicity Department, P.O. Box 1BQ, Robert Hyde House, 48 Bryanston Square, London W1H 1BQ.

Esso, ICI and Shell
These companies have film catalogues which include some excellent material, particularly about careers.

Unilever
Unilever publishes a series of four booklets called 'An introduction to business studies', covering business and society, marketing and management techniques. These are available from Unilever Educational Publications, P.O. Box 68, Unilever House, London EC4P 4BQ.

Company annual reports
Most large companies produce careers booklets and, often, illustrated annual reports. These contain information about their operation and products, together with their financial results which are useful as a basis for discussion. These are sometimes available on request in class sets.

HMSO
Fact sheets are available at a small cost on several aspects of industry from Her Majesty's Stationery Office.

Video Arts
Video Arts produce an excellent, simple and amusing film to explain profit and loss accounts, balance sheets and cash flow. It is called *The Balance-Sheet-Barrier*. Unfortunately it is not possible to rent this film, but a number of schools might be able to get together and buy it or to borrow it from a local company which uses it in training. Telephone 01-734 7671.

Trades Union Congress
The TUC publishes handbooks on trade union history and present day structure and function. These are available from Congress House, Great Russell Street, London WC1B 3LS.

Libraries
Local librarians can recommend reading on different aspects of industry.

In addition the following books and booklets are suggested for further reading.

General
Understanding Organisations, Charles B. Handy (Penguin)
Up the Organisation, Robert Townsend (Coronet)
Industry and Empire, E. J. Hobsbawn (Pelican)
The Multinationals, Christopher Tugendhat (Pelican)
The Business of Management, Roger Fack (Pelican)
Starting Work, Hilary Adamson and Mazzie Lewis (The Industrial Society)
The Work Challenge, John Garnett (The Industrial Society)
The Teachers' Treasure Chest, Schoolmaster Publishing Company (Exley Publications)
See Britain at Work, Angela Lansbury (Exley Publications)

Marketing
The Fundamentals and Practice of Marketing, John Wilmshurst (Heinemann)
Marketing, an Introductory Text, M. J. Baker (Macmillan)
Case Studies in Marketing, Charles Dunn (Papermac)
Retail Business Management, Gillespie: Hecht (McGraw Hill)
How to Advertise, K. Roman and J. Mass (Kogan Page)

Research, development and design
About Design, Ken Baynes (Design Council)
Let's Look at Design, C. G. Tomrley (Frederick Muller)
Design Education – Problem-solving and visual experience, Peter Green (Batsford)
Design in General Education, Edited by John Harahan (Design Council)

Manufacturing
Manufacturing Processes, Herbert W. Yankee (Prentice Hall)
Manufacturing Technology, G. Bram and C. Downs (Macmillan)
Production Engineering Technology, J. D. Radford and D. B. Richardson (Macmillan)
Manufacturing Technology, M. Hazelhurst (English Universities Press)
Production Decisions, John Powell, Understanding Business Series (Longman)

Finance
Money – whence it came where it went, J. K. Galbraith (Pelican)

Business Accounting 1, Frank Wood (Longman)
How the Stock Exchange Works, Norman Whetnall (Flame Books)
The Stock Exchange, free from the Information and Press Department, The Stock Exchange, London EC2N 1HP
A Career on the Stock Exchange, The Information and Press Department, The Stock Exchange, London EC2N 1HP

Personnel
A Textbook of Personnel Management, George Thomason (IPM)
The Practice of Personnel Management, David Barber (IPM)

Management Services
Work Study, W. Richardson, Secondary Science Series (Longman)
Teach Yourself Organisation and Methods, R. G. Breadmore (English Universities Press)
Organisation and Methods, R. G. Anderson, MandE Handbooks (Macdonald and Evans)
Industrial Management Services, H. Beeley, M and E Handbook (Macdonald and Evans)

Structure and size
Small is Beautiful, E. Schumacher (Fontana)

Motivation and money
The Human Side of Enterprise, D. McGregor (McGraw Hill)

Involvement: from communication to participation
Communication in Organisations, Lyman W. Porter and Karlene H. Roberts (Penguin)

Industrial relations and the trade union movement
Trade Unions, Edited by W. E. McCarthy (Penguin)
A History of Trade Unions, Henry Pelling (Pelican)

Industry and society
Why Industry Matters, Julia Cleverdon and Patrick Wintour (The Industrial Society)
Facts of Life, Richard Redden (Macdonald)
The Economic Facts of Life, Wilfred Sendall (Ibis Databank International Ltd)
Nationalised Industries, Graham L. Reid and Kevin Allen (Pelican)
A Guide to the British Economy, Peter Donaldson (Pelican)

Technology and change
The New Industrial State, J. K. Galbraith (Pelican)

Organisations

There are several organisations which are trying to encourage links between schools and industry and which can often provide useful literature and other assistance. Many of these are listed, with a full description of their activities, in a booklet called 'Schools and Industry' which is obtainable from CRAC.

Briefly these are:

The *Banking Information Service* which provides free resource material and arranges speakers for schools and colleges in order to help students to understand the part played by banks in a modern society, and to explain banking services.

Address: Banking Information Service, 10 Lombard Street, London EC3V 9AT. *Telephone:* 01-626 9386/7

The *Council of Engineering Institutions* which organises careers conventions, helps teachers to develop teaching material, assists with the 'Opening Windows' scheme which trains engineers to give talks to students, and generally aims to promote an understanding of engineering and its importance in modern industrial society.

Address: Council of Engineering Institutions, 2 Little Smith Street, Westminster, London SW1P 3DL. *Telephone:* 01-799 3912

The *CRAC Insight Programme* which organises courses and seminars to explain the creative and intellectually challenging demands of a management career and to help students to make more informed career decisions.

Address: CRAC Insight Programme, Careers Research and Advisory Centre, Bateman Street, Cambridge CB2 1LZ. *Telephone:* 0223-69811

The *Education for Industrial Society Challenge of Industry Conferences* which aim to increase sixth formers' understanding of the need to create wealth in industry and commerce and, secondly, of the vital challenge which exists today in managing and representing people at work.

Address: Education for Industrial Society, Robert Hyde House, 48 Bryanston Square, London W1H 1BQ. *Telephone:* 01-262-2401

The *Industry/Education Unit (Department of Industry)* which aims to improve attitudes to manufacturing industry among all young people through activities such as organising the Young Engineer for Britain competition, sponsoring a free film service for schools and encouraging other organisations involved in schools/ industry projects.

Address: Department of Industry, Industry/Education Unit, Ashdown House, 123 Victoria Street, London SW1E 6RB

The *Introduction to Industry Scheme for Teachers* which arranges for teachers to spend up to three weeks in industrial or commercial concerns to give them first hand experience of the world that many of their pupils will enter.

Address: Education, Training and Technology Directorate, Confederation of British Industry, Centre Point, 103 New Oxford St, London WC1A IDU. *Telephone:* 01379 7400

The *National Centre for School Technology* which runs training courses for teachers, produces teaching material, promotes resource-exchange schemes between industry and schools, and organises conferences and exhibitions. Its aim is to help teachers to make their work more relevant to the needs of a technological and industrial society.

Address: National Centre for School Technology, Trent Polytechnic, Burton Street, Nottingham NG1 4BU. *Telephone:* 0602-48248 Ext. 2182

Project Trident which, in association with local education authorities, co-ordinates projects providing work experience, voluntary community service and residential courses for those about to start work.

Address: Project Trident, Robert Hyde House, 48 Bryanston Square, London W1H 1BQ

The *School Technology Forum* which is made up of teachers' organisations. It encourages and helps those seeking to include matters relevant to technology in their classes, so that pupils may be better able to play full and active roles in a society increasingly dependent on technological factors and decisions.

Address: The Secretary, School Technology Forum, Trent Polytechnic, Burton Street, Nottingham NG1 4BU. *Telephone:* 0602-48248

The *Schools Council Industry Project*, conducted in conjunction with the CBI and TUC, investigates ways in which the nature of modern industrial society can be introduced into the school curriculum.

Address: Schools Council Industry Project, 160 Great Portland Street, London W1N 6LL. *Telephone:* 01-580 0352

The *Schools—Industry Link Scheme* which produces Resource Directories to guide teachers on the resources available to them from local industry, to facilitate the formation of links between schools and industry.

Address: Schools—Industry Link Scheme, The Polytechnic of North London, Holloway Road, London N7 8DB. *Telephone:* 01-607 2789

The *Schools Information Centre on the Chemical Industry* which offers a range of free publications and other materials to provide schools with up to date information about the chemical and allied industries.

Address: Dr Barbara Haines, Schools Information Centre on the Chemical Industry, The Polytechnic of North London, Holloway Road, London N7 8DB. *Telephone:* 01-607 2789 Ext. 2157

The *Science and Technology Regional Organisations (SATROs)* are spread throughout the country and are involved in a number of activities including producing newsletters and reports, sponsoring courses, promoting project work in schools and establishing contact between schools and industry. They aim to encourage innovation in science and technology education; to improve understanding between schools and industry and to provide practical help to teachers.

Address: The Executive Secretary, SCSST, 1 Birdcage Walk, London SW1H 9JJ. *Telephone:* 01-222 7899

The *Standing Conference on Schools' Science and Technology* which brings together educational, industrial, professional and governmental interests at national level in order to improve the teaching of science and technology in schools and to encourage closer relationships between schools and industry.

Address: as for SATRO

The *Trades Union Congress Education Department* which assists trade union representatives who are invited to talk in schools, to discuss their experiences as active trade unionists and the role of the trade union movement. It also helps teachers in preparing materials to introduce young people to industrial society and the requirements of working life.

Address: Education Department, Trades Union Congress, Congress House, Great Russell Street, London WC1B 3LS. *Telephone:* 01-636 4030

Understanding British Industry which encourages relationships between schools and local companies by means of well-prepared visits, speakers, lending of facilities, equipment and so on, and promoting training of teachers through secondments to industrial and commercial firms. UBI deals with the 13—16 year old school age group.

Addresses: Understanding British Industry, The CBI Education Foundation, Centre Point, 103 New Oxford St, London WC1A 1DU *Telephone:* 01 379 7400 Understanding British Industry, Sun Alliance House, New Inn Hall Street, Oxford OX1 2QE. *Telephone:* 0865-722585

Young Enterprise which provides pupils with the opportunity to set up and run their own scale-model company on commercial lines from incorporation to liquidation. This aims to educate them in the organisation, methods and practice of commerce and industry.

Address: Young Enterprise, Robert Hyde House, 48 Bryanston Square, London W1H 1BQ *Telephone:* 01-

In addition you might contact your local chamber of commerce and professional bodies such as the Institute of Personnel Management, the Institute of Marketing and the Institution of Production Engineers.

Activities

The following activities may help to make your discussions on industry more interesting and give a further insight into how companies work.

(1) Organise visits to local businesses and look at the way they are run. How are they structured? Where are their markets? How does management communicate and consult with the employees? To which unions to their employees belong?
(2) Visit your local authority's offices to look at the structure plan for the area. How many people are employed by local companies? How does this compare with the numbers working in local government and the social services? What does it cost each year to finance your school or local hospital? How does this compare with the money earned by industry in the same area?
(3) Conduct a market survey in the high street on the images of local companies. How are they regarded? . . . as a necessary evil? . . . as a vital asset?
(4) Invite people working in industry to speak at your school. It is important to hear first hand what it is like to be, for example, a company accountant or a personnel clerk or a shop steward.

It would also be extremely useful to ask people from a local company to participate in working on some of the case studies in this book. Their experience could make the discussion far more meaningful. In particular, it would be a good idea to ask the financial manager of a local company to assist with the financial case studies and business games.

(5) Spend time in companies whenever possible, perhaps doing holiday jobs or projects, so that you can see the work described in the book actually happening and the decisions being made.

Index